The four papers comprising this volume were prepared under the 1989 "Socio-economic Aspects of Climate Change" activity of the OECD Environment Committee. This report is published under the responsibility of the Secretary-General.

Funding support was provided by the U.S. Environmental Protection Agency for the Johnson chapter. The special assistance provided by Martin Parry and Edmund Penning-Rowsell in the development of the Sonka and Jansen *et al.* chapters is also gratefully acknowledged.

Also available

THE STATE OF THE ENVIRONMENT & Supplement: Environmental Indicators –
A Preliminary Set (1991)
(97 91 01 1) ISBN 92–64–13442–5   £22.00   US$38.00 FF180   DM70

ECONOMIC INSTRUMENTS FOR ENVIRONMENTAL PROTECTION(1989)
(97 89 04 1) ISBN 92–64–13251–1   £13.50   US$23.50 FF110   DM46

ENERGY TECHNOLOGIES FOR REDUCING EMISSIONS OF GREENHOUSE GASES.
VOLUME 1 – VOLUME 2. Proceedings of an Experts' Seminar, Paris 12th–14th April 1989
(1989)*
(61 89 09 1) ISBN 92–64–13267–8   £48.00   US$84.00 FF400   DM164

*Two Volumes not sold separately

ENVIRONMENTAL POLICY BENEFITS: MONETARY VALUATION (1989)
(97 88 07 1) ISBN 92–64–13182–5   £11.50   US$20.00 FF95   DM39

ENVIRONMENTAL POLICY AND TECHNICAL CHANGE (1985)
(97 85 07 1) ISBN 92–64–12731–3   £9.00   US$18.00 FF90   DM40

Prices charged at the OECD Bookshop.
The OECD CATALOGUE OF PUBLICATIONS and supplements will be sent free of charge
on request addressed either to OECD Publications Service,
2, rue André–Pascal, 75775 PARIS CEDEX 16,
or to the OECD Distributor in your country

Climate Change

EVALUATING THE SOCIO-ECONOMIC IMPACTS

ORGANISATION FOR ECONOMIC CO-OPERATION AND DEVELOPMENT

Pursuant to Article 1 of the Convention signed in Paris on 14th December 1960, and which came into force on 30th September 1961, the Organisation for Economic Co-operation and Development (OECD) shall promote policies designed:

- to achieve the highest sustainable economic growth and employment and a rising standard of living in Member countries, while maintaining financial stability, and thus to contribute to the development of the world economy;
- to contribute to sound economic expansion in Member as well as non-member countries in the process of economic development; and
- to contribute to the expansion of world trade on a multilateral, non-discriminatory basis in accordance with international obligations.

The original Member countries of the OECD are Austria, Belgium, Canada, Denmark, France, Germany, Greece, Iceland, Ireland, Italy, Luxembourg, the Netherlands, Norway, Portugal, Spain, Sweden, Switzerland, Turkey, the United Kingdom and the United States. The following countries became Members subsequently through accession at the dates indicated hereafter: Japan (28th April 1964), Finland (28th January 1969), Australia (7th June 1971) and New Zealand (29th May 1973). The Commission of the European Communities takes part in the work of the OECD (Article 13 of the OECD Convention). Yugoslavia takes part in some of the work of the OECD (agreement of 28th October 1961).

Publié en français sous le titre :

LE CHANGEMENT
CLIMATIQUE
ÉVALUATION DES RETOMBÉES
SOCIO-ÉCONOMIQUES

TABLE OF CONTENTS

Chapter 1

EVALUATING THE SOCIO-ECONOMIC IMPACTS OF CLIMATE CHANGE: AN INTRODUCTION

David Pearce*

Although the science remains uncertain, 1990 marked the year when many governments accepted the impending reality of global climate change. Some governments began to announce targets for reductions in carbon dioxide in order to prompt the international negotiation process. Some governments remain unconvinced that the greenhouse effect is real. Others accept the science, but not the need to act dramatically. This volume is concerned not with the scientific debate as such, but with the basis for climate change policy in OECD countries. Crucial to the whole process of policy development is an assessment of the impacts of climate change.

These impacts will appear first as physical changes in the environment, but will eventually translate into social and economic changes as well. Impacts are important, essentially because they represent the potential benefits that might be realised from taking political action against the climate change problem. If impacts are projected to be small, or if it is likely that the forecasted impacts could be easily managed, then the benefits of measures to contain global warming will be small, and the balance of costs and benefits will militate against major policy action. On the other hand, if the impacts are projected to be large, or if there is a real risk of some of them taking on "catastrophic" proportions, then early and firm action would be prudent. Put another way, the cost-benefit balance, however imperfectly understood, is fundamental to the policy process.

Because the costs of environmental policy are typically easier to quantify than the benefits, policy discussions often begin with an exogenously-determined "target", and seek to minimise the costs of achieving that target. This is more cost-effectiveness analysis than it is cost-benefit analysis. It has the advantage of being conceptually simpler, but it runs the risk that the initial target will be inappropriately set. If this target is too stringent (or not stringent enough), there is a likelihood that both economic and environmental resources will

---

* David Pearce is Professor of Economics at University College London, Director of the London Environmental Economics Centre, and Special Advisor to the UK Secretary of State for the Environment. He has taught at the Universities of Lancaster, Southampton, Leicester and Aberdeen, as well as the University of Adelaide, before taking up his UCL post in 1983.

be "wasted". Given the long time horizons involved in the climate change issue, and given the world-wide economic and environmental implications of that issue, the potential for such wastage is very high indeed. It is a basic premise of this book that economic resources should be allocated to resolving the climate change problem (i.e. costs should be incurred) only to the extent that the benefits (i.e. reduced damages potential) warrant these costs. In order to define this "tradeoff" point, an effort has to be made to measure the potential impacts of global warming.

OVERVIEW OF PRESENT SITUATION

The Intergovernmental Panel on Climate Change (IPCC) was set up by the United Nations Environment Programme (UNEP) and the World Meteorological Organisation (WMO) in 1988 to investigate global warming. It established three working groups to help it fulfil its mandate. Working Group 1 (Chaired by the United Kingdom) has looked at the scientific evidence in support of global warming. Working Group 2 (chaired by the Soviet Union) has investigated potential impacts. Working Group 3 (chaired by the United States) has evaluated various policy response options.

Global Warming Scenarios

Working Group 1 has forecast that global warming will indeed occur, and has assessed four possible scenarios:

Scenario A: "Business as usual" i.e. a continuation of current trends in greenhouse gas emissions, which will produce a rate of warming in terms of global mean surface temperatures of 0.2°C –0.5°C per decade in the 21st century, with a "best guess" of 0.3°C. This would produce a 1 degree rise in temperature by 2025 and 3 degrees by 2100, compared to 1990 levels.

Scenario B: Deforestation is halted, natural gas is increasingly substituted for coal, energy conservation occurs, but temperatures still rise by 2°C by 2100 compared to today, i.e. a rise of 0.2°C per decade.

Scenario C: A greater switch to renewable energy sources in the second half of the 21st century holds the temperature rise to a little above 0.1°C per decade.

Scenario D: Assumes that the switch to renewables occurs in the first half of the 21st century, which stabilises gas concentrations in the atmosphere.

The scenarios are shown in Figure 1. The temperatures in question are global mean temperatures. For policy purposes, these estimates are not very useful. What matters more is the regional variation which will exist around about the mean. For example, in the "business as usual" scenario, temperatures are expected to be higher than the mean in Southern Europe and central North America, with reduced summer rainfall and soil moisture. By 2030, winter temperatures could rise in these regions by 2°C (perhaps more in Central North America), and summer temperatures by 2-3°C. In the Sahel, warming will

Figure 1. **GLOBAL TEMPERATURE CHANGE THREE SCENARIOS**

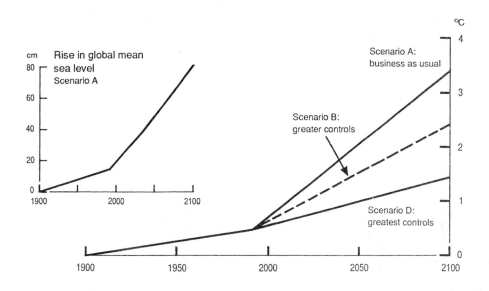

Source: IPCC

increase by 1-3°C. South East Asia might experience temperature rises of 1-2°C, and Australia some 1-2°C in summer and 2°C in winter.

Sea levels rise in the "business as usual" scenario by some 6 cms per decade due to thermal expansion of the oceans, and the melting of some land ice, producing a rise of some 20 cms by 2030, and 65 cms by 2100.

Regional Shares of Emissions

Table 1 illustrates the relative contributions of the world's regions to greenhouse gas emissions. The importance of the USA and USSR/Eastern Europe are clearly seen, as is the role of European Community countries (which make up the bulk of the "rest of OECD"). The rapid growth of the developing countries' shares is also seen - note the very rapid rise in the share of Centrally Planned Asia (China mainly), and other developing countries. Any agreement on emission controls must, therefore, secure the co-operation of both developed and developing countries, if it is to be successful.

Impacts

The Working Group 2 report emphasises the fact that uncertainty is a major problem to be overcome in assessing the socio-economic impacts of climate change. Given the large

11

Table 1. **Regional contributions to Greenhouse Gas Emissions**

CO₂ Anthropogenic Emissions Shares (%)				
Source	1985	2000	2015	2050
United States	21	19	16	12
Rest of OECD	22	19	16	12
USSR and Eastern Europe	22	22	19	18
Centrally Planned Asia	10	13	16	21
Other Developing Countries	25	28	32	37
Commercial Energy	86	87	89	92
Tropical Deforestation	12	11	9	6
Other	2	2	2	2
Total (10^9 tonnes Carbon)	5.99	8.05	10.27	16.95
Average Annual Growth Rate		1.6 %		

Methane Anthropogenic Emissions Shares (%)				
Source	1985	2000	2015	2050
United States	12	11	9	8
Rest of OECD	13	12	12	10
USSR and Eastern Europe	13	14	14	15
Other Developing Countries	17	16	17	19
Other Developing Countries	46	47	49	48
Fuel Production	18	22	26	32
Enteric Fermentation	23	24	23	22
Rice Cultivation	34	31	29	24
Landfills	9	10	10	14
Tropical Deforestation	6	6	5	4
Other	9	7	7	
Total (10^5 tonnes CH₄)	320.1	399.5	476.8	710.5
Average Annual Growth Rate		1.2 %		

uncertainties that are involved, it is understandable that most of the impacts described in their report are outlined in qualitative terms only. Nevertheless, Working Group 2 foresees significant impacts in virtually all economic sectors, assuming that temperatures and sea levels rise as predicted. More specifically, Working Group 2 recommends that efforts should be intensified to better understand the linkages between physical and socio-economic impacts, and that better methodologies for quantifying these impacts need to be developed. To some extent, this conclusion is based on the three methodological studies contained in this book. Working Group 2 recognised early in its mandate that hard data on the impacts of climate change simply does not exist. Some studies had been carried out on potential *physical* impacts, but virtually no guidance existed on the possible "downstream" social, and economic response functions. For that reason, Working Group 2 asked OECD to work on developing "more robust" methodologies for assessing these types of impact. The papers presented in this book are a direct response to this request.

12

Policy Options

How should the international community respond to the issue of global warming? Working Group 3 points out that there are basically three options:

i) Do Nothing

The arguments for doing nothing are:
- That global warming is all very uncertain anyway;
- That doing something may be expensive and that costs borne today will benefit generations yet to come (an inequitable situation);
- That delaying present action will improve the level of scientific information about global warming; and
- That the world will adapt "automatically" through migration, changing agricultural production, switching expenditures to sea level defences, and so on.

The arguments against doing nothing are:
- That global warming is irreversible. The longer the delay, the more warming the world is committed to. If the worst fears are realised, it will be too late to correct it;
- That scientific information can be improved even while further action is being considered;
- That delay is "intergenerationally unfair" - current generations have an obligation not to impose heavy costs on future generations; and
- That action now could be relatively cheap (e.g. energy conservation), and will likely yield other environmental benefits (e.g. reduced acid rain; reduced congestion, if the contribution of road travel to CO_2 is properly tackled, etc.).

ii) Reduce Emissions and Invest in Carbon "Sinks"

The arguments for reducing emissions are very much the same as the arguments against doing nothing. The additional advantage of acting to reduce the problem at source is that it gives greater certainty compared to adaptation policies (see below). Most importantly, global warming may have a large potential for "surprise" events, e.g. major climatic incidents, simply because we know so little about how climatic systems function. These surprises may be very damaging. By reducing emissions, we lower the potential for unpleasant surprises.

The obvious argument against reducing greenhouse gas (GHG) emissions is that, while it may be fairly cheap in the short run, further reductions in emissions will get more and more expensive. A number of studies have estimated costs of adjustment, and some have suggested that major reductions in GHGs could be very costly in economic terms[1].

Afforestation offers the potential for "fixing" CO_2, although due allowance has to be made for carbon release once the forest rotation has ended and the wood decays. Much depends on how the wood is used. For example, wood for paper pulp would release carbon fairly quickly, or would contribute to methane releases in landfill sites. Wood used for furniture and building could store carbon for much longer. Afforestation in the tropics might fix carbon on an even bigger scale.

Afforestation also introduces the idea of "carbon offsets". An electric power utility might be allowed to build a new power station, provided it "offset" the projected emissions with carbon-fixing trees. Since it does not matter where the emissions and fixing take place (in terms of global warming), the prospect is opened up for tropical afforestation as an offset to increased carbon emissions in the rich world. This is already happening. One US utility has agreed to conserve tropical forest in Guatemala. Dutch utilities may well plant new forests in Colombia, Ecuador and Peru.

The arguments against afforestation as a "cure" are:

- It could be very expensive;
- Much modern afforestation is regarded as being environmentally unattractive anyway (e.g. conifer plantations); and
- In order to overcome the problem of merely postponing carbon releases (because of wood decay), afforestation would have to proceed at a faster and faster pace over time.

iii)   Invest in Adaptation

Under the "do nothing" option, adaptation is "natural": it simply comes about because people respond to climatic change. But governments could also invest in adaptation by e.g. raising existing sea defences and building new ones; investing in new research and development (e.g. more climate resistant crops); protecting groundwater systems from salinisation; relocating communities; etc.

The argument for adaptation is that it may be a lot cheaper than emission reduction, especially if costs could be spread out over very long periods of time. The argument against adaptation is that it does nothing to reduce further warming, and simply imposes bigger and bigger cost burdens on future generations. Although it is illustrative to fix our attention on certain threshold points in time (e.g. the year in which CO_2 emission levels are expected to reach twice their current magnitude), it should not be forgotten that warming will continue long beyond this point, if no action is taken.

Choosing a Policy Mix

In the end, international global warming policy will probably consist of some measure of all three of these options. In particular:

- Some warming will be allowed to take place, simply because the economic dislocation caused by aiming for stabilisation of temperature is likely to be too great;
- Because some warming will take place, both "natural" and "engineered" adaptations will occur;
- The international community is already focusing on emission reduction (coupled with afforestation) as its primary policy response. From the discussion above, it is clear that, so long as the welfare of future generations matters, this is a sensible approach.

TWO APPROACHES TO SETTING EMISSION TARGETS: "COST-BENEFIT" VERSUS "MINIMUM SURPRISE"

How should a global warming target be set? IPCC Working Group I has suggested that the world should aim to limit the rate of warming to 0.1°C to 0.2°C centigrade per decade: in other words, a 1-2°C rise in mean global temperature in the next 100 years.

The rationale for this target is based on risk aversion, or, more accurately, "minimum surprise". The idea is that beyond the 0.1-0.2°C per decade rate of warming, we are very unsure what will happen. Higher rates of increase would take the world beyond the projected capacity of its major ecosystems to adapt without catastrophic change. Within this rate of increase, it is reasonably certain that impacts, while they will still exist, will be within existing management capabilities. In terms of Figure 2, the "damage curve" becomes an unknown beyond a 0.1°C rate of warming, and moves into the "zone of potential surprise".

IPCC tend to suggest that the upper end of this target (0.2°C) will require firm action on CFCs and other non-carbon GHGs, as well as on stabilising CO_2 emissions at their 1990 level by the turn of the century. Allowing for the projected growth in CO_2 emissions between now and 2000, this is equivalent to cutting emissions in 2000 or 2005 by around 20 per cent.

As indicated above, there is an alternative way of setting a global warming target. This approach would use cost-benefit analysis.

Basically, abating emissions now costs money because resources have to be diverted into things such as energy conservation rather than spending them elsewhere on more "productive" uses. Or, people's choices have to be restricted, again implying an economic cost. On one side of the picture, then, we have abatement costs. But there are benefits of abatement as well, and these will show up as avoided damage, e.g. avoided costs of

Figure 2. **THE MINIMUM SURPRISE APPROACH TO WARMING TARGETS**

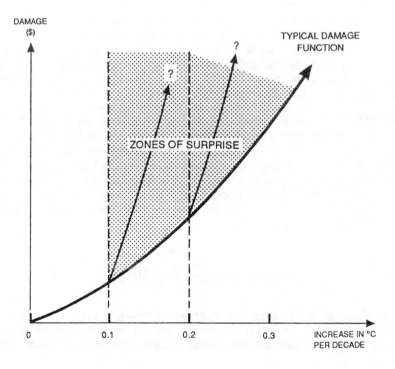

15

adaptation such as sea defence expenditures, avoided dislocation to agriculture, and so on. These are the abatement benefits.

The aim of cost-benefit analysis would be to identify that rate of warming which gives the greatest difference between abatement benefits and abatement costs, the highest level of net benefits. This rate can then be translated into a target for emission reductions. Identifying this target means setting marginal abatement costs equal to marginal abatement benefits. Although it is obviously extremely difficult to carry out such an exercise, one recent study has attempted such a rough cost-benefit calculation[2]. Under a "do nothing" scenario, this study suggests that the world would face a damage bill of somewhere between 0.2 per cent and 2.4 per cent of the entire global income in around 100 years time. The range reflects a judgmental assessment of the uncertainty in the estimates. This translates to a damage cost per tonne of CO_2[3] of somewhere between \$3.3 and \$36.9. The damages estimated are mainly in the form of market-related costs, e.g. the costs of damage due to sea level rise. In terms of the recommended size of emission reductions, the study concludes that:

- CFCs should be phased out completely;
- CO_2 should be reduced by 10-30 per cent on the levels that would otherwise obtain in the year 2050.

Interestingly, the cost-benefit approach is compatible with the risk-aversion approach in terms of its recommendation to phase out CFCs, but its CO_2 reduction target is very much lower than what is suggested by the risk-aversion approach. (Recall that that approach suggested a 20 per cent reduction on 2000/2005 levels, compared to the cost-benefit finding that a similar reduction is required, but based on 2050 levels). Thus, the risk-aversion approach appears to suggest much more demanding reductions in GHGs than does the cost-benefit approach.

However, there are conceptual deficiencies associated with both approaches. For example, the risk-aversion approach ignores the costs of abatement altogether, and assumes that the damage done from entering the "zone of ignorance" will be extremely large. On the other hand, the cost-benefit approach tends to ignore the potential for "surprise" events such as changes in the frequency and severity of droughts, floods, storms and frosts. It also often ignores the "incidental" benefits of reducing GHGs, e.g. in the form of reduced acid rain, noise and road congestion. One study, for Norway[4], suggests that a policy of stabilising emission levels at the projected level for the year 2000 would cost Norway some 27 billion krone in foregone GDP in 2010 (about 2.7 per cent of 2010 GDP). The incidental benefits would amount to about 19 billion krone, so that the issue becomes one of judging whether the "deficit" of 8 billion krone is outweighed by the political gains from taking action as a means of encouraging global action. Finally, it should be pointed out that, if the cost-benefit approach could capture all potential impacts, it would not differ from the risk aversion approach. However, this is quite different from saying that the IPCC interpretation of the risk-aversion approach is correct.

TREATING UNCERTAINTY

The "minimum surprise" approach adopts an extremely cautious attitude to the "zone of ignorance" in Figure 2. This zone is larger the greater the uncertainties associated with global warming become. What are the sources of these uncertainties? They include:

Uncertainty About Trace Gas Emissions

The relative contributions of the different GHGs to global warming depend on the time horizons used, since different gases have different 'lives' in the atmosphere. IPCC's concept of "global warming potential" (GWP) attempts to capture these differences. Relative GWPs, using a 100 year time horizon, as outlined by the IPCC, are illustrated in Table 2. The sources of these gases are many, ranging from fossil fuel combustion and deforestation for CO_2, to rice paddies and livestock for methane, and nitrogen fertilisers for N_2O, among others. It follows that projecting GHG emissions requires detailed modelling of the sources and their expected rates of change over time. However, CO_2 and methane obviously dominate the totals, with the former being derived mainly from fossil fuel combustion. Accurately forecasting GHG emissions therefore depends very heavily on forecasts of energy use over time, including forecasts of the composition of the various energy sources.

Table 2. **Relative Contributions to "Global Warming Potential"**

	GWP	1990 Emissions (trillion grams)	Relative contribution over 100 years(%)
CO_2	1	26,000	66
Methane	21	300	16.5
N_2O	290	6	4.5
CFC_{11}	3 500	0.3	(12)
CFC_{12}	7 300	0.4	
$HCFC_{22}$	1 500	0.1	0.5
Other			0.5

Source: IPCC.

Uncertainty About Climate Response

How the climate will respond to the various "doses" of GHGs is also uncertain. The effects of feedback mechanisms are disputed. Thus, global warming should increase the amount of water vapour taken up from the oceans, leading to cloud formation. But the effects of clouds on warming are uncertain. They could increase or decrease warming according to whether their "sunshade" effect or their "blanket" effect dominates (the sunshade effect reflects the sun's heat back into space, the blanket effect reflects back heat radiated from the earth).

Uncertainty About Regional Impacts

Existing global circulation models (GCMs) do not yet have the capacity to predict regional climate change: the finest grid spacing in current models relates to an area about the size of France. Yet, for socio-economic impact assessment, it is the regional impacts that matter, not changes in global mean temperatures.

Threshold Uncertainty

The existence of thresholds has already been alluded to. The "zone of surprise" in Figure 2 implies that the damage function related to global warming may be discontinuous. If so, it is of considerable importance to identify thresholds and to avoid them if they clearly have major damage implications. But, beyond the general statement that surprises may be in store at rates of warming above 0.1-0.2°C threshold per decade, this field of study is not very well-advanced.

Uncertainty About Social Response

There are two major sources of uncertainty relating to the way in which societies will respond to climate change. These are:

a) The degree to which "natural adaptation" will occur; and
b) The extent and nature of government response.

Since a good deal of the effects of climate change will be gradual, individuals and societies will respond more or less automatically by making adaptations in the ways they relate to their environments. Such changes could include population migrations, modifications of consumption patterns, incurring "defensive expenditures" against the increased risk of floods and weather events, modifying crop mixes, and so on. It is important to understand that, while "natural adaptation" corresponds to the normal concept of "do nothing" scenarios, such adaptation is not costless. Essentially, individuals will bear costs they would otherwise have not incurred.

The level and type of government response is also uncertain. Initially, governments are likely to engage in a mix of adaptation and prevention. The former, however, is very much under the control of individual governments, whereas prevention is unlikely to occur, on any significant scale anyway, unless there is global or near-global agreement to reduce GHG emissions. This observation is critical, for it means that policy prescription is itself dependent upon the chances of global agreement. Otherwise, individual governments are unlikely to act unilaterally. The possibility of achieving such a global agreement can best be analysed in terms of "game theory" models, i.e. by looking at the costs and benefits to each country of joining an international agreement, and then at the incentives that it would be necessary to provide to secure agreement from those who stand to be "net losers" from the agreement (i.e. those who are net gainers from doing nothing or from only undertaking adaptation policies).

CONCLUSIONS: TOWARDS A GLOBAL CLIMATE POLICY

The global warming problem presents a fundamental challenge for international environmental policy. Its critical features are:

Scientific uncertainty about the existence of a "greenhouse effect", compounded by uncertainties about the scale of damage and its incidence in time and space. The traditional cost-benefit methodology clearly has an important role to play, but it is important to note that several features of the climate issue challenge some of the basic assumptions of such models.

First, the uncertainty will often be of a form that does not permit the prior assignment of probabilities to outcomes, and the uncertainty will often be about major damage events. We suggested earlier that this could be characterised by the "zone of potential surprise" concept. This suggests that a decision-theoretic framework might be more appropriate than a probabilistic one.

Second, the changes that may occur may be "non-marginal", i.e. of significant size and with the potential for disrupting some economies at a large scale. Cost-benefit analysis is essentially about marginal changes in variables.

Third, cost-benefit analysis will also require that "least cost" solutions be found, i.e. that any policy aimed at a given target be achieved at least resource cost. In turn, this suggests a mix of adaptation and prevention, but, as yet, the nature of this (optimum) mix is unclear. Moreover, what is 'least-cost' today may be unfair to future generations. Suppose, for example, that adaptation is cheaper than prevention for current generations, and that the effect of discounting maintains that difference into the future. Then (more) adaptation may be chosen over (more) prevention. But adaptation bequeaths increased global warming (which may be irreversible) to subsequent generations. The impact of discounting could, as is well known, lead to intergenerationally unfair solutions.

Fourth, cost-benefit assumes that most, though not all, impacts are subject to valuation. Valuation is difficult enough in localised impact studies, but global impacts are notoriously difficult to estimate. Many of the problems will not arise out of monetary valuation as such, but from the difficulty of knowing what the "dose-response" functions actually are, i.e. what impacts will occur. The pervasive uncertainty of global warming largely explains this problem - models cannot yet identify regional impacts accurately, and all kinds of general equilibrium and social responses will ultimately take place to modify the impacts. In the absence of credible valuation techniques, decision rules become "fuzzy" and polar extremes are likely to emerge in the policy debate. Indeed, this phenomenon is already occurring.

The ultimate challenge of global warming, however, is that the combination of uncertainty, irreversibility and the impact on future generations means that policy-making is very likely to "run ahead" of the natural, economic and social science needed to inform that policy-making. Indeed, there are many signs that this is already happening. If climate change really does threaten major surprises or significant, but unsurprising, damage, then action now is warranted. But this action needs to be efficient. However imperfectly, costs and benefits must be considered, and least-cost options chosen. It seems fair to say that, as of now, we do not have adequate information to guide this process with a measurable degree of confidence in the reliability of the advice. "More research" and "more information" is one inevitable response to such a situation. It is not likely to satisfy those who want "real" action, but it is a highly sensible response. After that, there is a powerful case for adopting low-cost warming-prevention strategies which have other benefits as well. Then, if the greenhouse effect turns out to be a "non-event", nothing has been lost. In fact, there will even likely have been environmental gains. Only after these (relatively easy) policy decisions have been taken will the "hard debate" about global warming policy begin. At that point, it will be vital to have much better feel for the impacts of global warming, and the various ways in which the world's economies might respond to those impacts.

More specifically, this means:

i) Developing models that bridge the gap between physical and economic impacts;
ii) Developing a better understanding of likely adaptive and preventive policy options, and how these "feed back" to projected impacts over time;

iii) Understanding the boundaries between the many uncertainties that are involved, with particular emphasis on the potential for catastrophe (e.g. environmental extinctions); and

iv) Developing decision-theoretic models, based on reasonably credible estimates of both the benefits and the costs of alternative policy options.

In this volume, an attempt has been made to clarify some of these issues for two key policy areas: agriculture and sea level rise. Obviously, these are not the only critical impact assessment sectors. There are also important impacts likely to be experienced in forests, oceans, drylands, etc., assuming the kinds of climatic change scenarios that Working Group 1 has analysed. The intent here is merely to use the agriculture and sea level rise issues as examples to point the way to improved impact assessment methodologies in general. As noted above, considerably more study will be necessary to actually quantify these impacts for specific locations.

Each of the three studies presented in the following sections (agriculture; agricultural trade; and sea level rise) provides suggestions for specific improvements in impact assessment methodologies for its own area of interest. Taken together, they are intended to serve as a modest contribution to the important goal of better economic analysis of the impacts of climate change.

NOTES

1. See, notably, A. MANNE AND R. RICHELS (forthcoming), "CO_2 Emission Limits: An Economic Cost Analysis for the USA", *The Energy Journal*. This study estimates a cost to the USA of \$3.6 trillion to achieve a permanent 20 per cent reduction in 1990 emission levels.

2. See W. NORDHAUS (1990), "To Slow or Not to Slow: The Economics of the Greenhouse Effect", Department of Economics, Yale University, *Mimeo*. The Nordhaus study does not estimate "incidental" benefits (from reductions in other pollutants) from GHG reduction. One study that *does* attempt this is S. GLOMSROD *et al.*, (1990), *Stabilisation of Emissions of CO_2: A Computable General Equilibrium Assessment'*, Central Bureau of Statistics, Oslo.

3. Actually, of CO_2 equivalent, since the study allows for other GHGs, and converts them to CO_2 equivalents.

4. GLOMSROD, *op. cit.*

20

Chapter 2

METHODOLOGICAL GUIDELINES FOR ASSESSING THE SOCIO-ECONOMIC IMPACTS OF CLIMATE CHANGE ON AGRICULTURE

Steven Sonka*

INTRODUCTION

The build-up of greenhouse gases in the environment, and the changes in the global climate that are expected to result from that build-up, are increasingly being recognised as issues of urgent international concern. Led by the United Nations, the world is now beginning to seriously examine the potential environmental, socio-economic and policy response impacts of global climate change. In particular, the UNEP/WMO Intergovernmental Panel on Climate Change (IPCC) has recently established three international Working Groups to deal explicitly with each of these three broad topics.

Although much of the climate change research effort to date has focused on the environmental changes that might take place, there is a growing awareness of the need to develop an understanding of the socio-economic impacts as well. In effect, it will be important to understand not only how the global climate is changing, but also how these changes impact on our economies and on our societies in general. Without this "higher order" understanding, it is unlikely that the eventual policy response(s) to climate change will be optimal.

There has been some preliminary work done on assessing socio-economic impacts, but this work is still in the early stages of development. IPCC Working Group 2 recognised early in its mandate that a full socio-economic impact assessment would be hindered by the lack of a clear impact assessment methodology.

As part of its own contribution to Working Group 2, OECD, therefore, undertook to help in the development of such a methodology. To that end, it was agreed that OECD would consolidate available literature and suggest improved methodological guidelines for these key impact areas – agriculture, agricultural trade and sea-level rise. This paper presents the results of the agricultural sector review.

---

* Steven Sonka is Professor of Agricultural Management at the University of Illinois at Urbana-Champaign. He is also a partner in Agricultural Education and Consulting, a business and financial management consulting firm based in Champaign, Illinois.

OBJECTIVES

This paper is concerned with development of an improved methodology for assessing the socio-economic impacts of climate change on the agricultural sector. Its specific objectives are:

a) To review key literature assessing the agricultural impacts of climate change to ascertain the "state-of-the-art" methodologies currently employed.
b) To document the extent to which critical concerns (such as uncertainty, regionalisation, and sensitivity of conclusions) have been addressed in prior work.
c) To make concrete suggestions for improving the existing agricultural impact assessment methodology.

It is not intended that the recommendations contained in this paper will constitute a comprehensive methodology in themselves – instead they are provided as useful steps toward that goal. But it is hoped that OECD countries will find these suggestions practical and useful for guiding future research on agricultural impact assessment within their jurisdictions.

PERSPECTIVE

"Methodology – a body of methods, rules, and postulates employed by a discipline; a particular procedure or set of procedures" (Webster's, 1970, p. 533).

Specification of a particular set of procedures as "preferred" implies general agreement as to the purpose driving the underlying analyses. It appears that the underlying purpose is still evolving for agricultural impact assessments of climate change (AIACC). As will be documented later, most prior studies have served a very narrow purpose. That purpose was generally to point out that a changed climate could have profound consequences for the agricultural production system.

From a decision-making perspective, however, demonstrating potential effects has limited usefulness. Instead, decision-makers need information which will aid in problem identification, evaluation of alternative actions, and/or selection of preferred responses. This paper will adopt a decision- making perspective. Doing so reflects the assumption that future AIACCs will be driven by the need for societal decision-makers to make a number of difficult choices.

This section of the paper describes three critically important aspects of the decision perspective as it relates to climate change. First, two key realities of the manner by which climate affects the agricultural system are outlined. Building upon this description, the types and characteristics of decision-makers who are the major audiences of AIACC are then identified. The final component of this section summarises the three major social issues which face agricultural policy-makers. The ultimate justification for conducting AIACC's is to provide information to assist decision-makers in addressing these issues.

A Simplified Impacts Model

The methodology for analysing AIACC must reflect the manner in which climate change actually affects the agricultural economy and the broader society. Two critically important aspects of that process are *1)* geographic scale interactions within the system and *2)* temporal linkages from one production period to the next (Sonka and Lamb, 1987). Geographic scale linkages will be addressed first.

Figure 1 provides an abbreviated description of those linkages. There, climate change is depicted as first affecting agriculture at very micro levels; for example, a warmer summer growing season directly impacts microprocesses within plants and animals, properties of the soil, and pests within the agricultural setting. These influences are integrated as they affect yields of individual plants and animals. As also noted in Figure 1, environmental effects occur at both physical and biological levels.

These direct effects are further integrated at the level of the farm firm within the profit potential of that unit. The individual producer will respond to the altered productivity that a change in climate provides. Management actions will be taken to mitigate (exploit) the unfavourable (beneficial) aspects of climate change. These actions include changes to existing production processes and enterprise choices using current technology as well as the search for new technologies. These adaptations in turn have potential environmental implications as well as potential effects for the economic activities that support the agricultural production system.

Figure 1. **SCHEMATIC ILLUSTRATING KEY GEOGRAPHIC SCALE LINKAGES WITHIN THE AGRICULTURAL SECTOR**

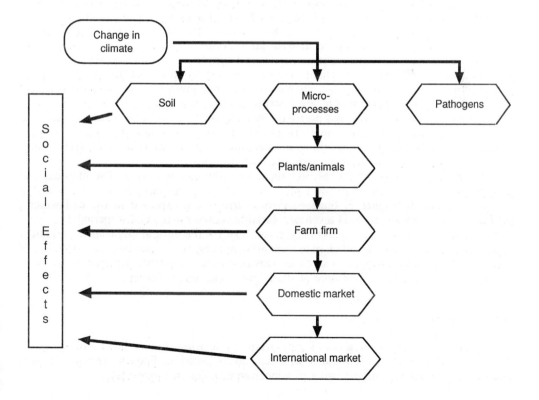

Of course, climate change will affect not only a single producer. Therefore, the effects of the changed climate and of associated producer adaptations need to be considered at a more aggregate level. For exposition purposes, these are noted as domestic market effects in Figure 1. Here, the aggregate effects are expressed in terms of physical food production and consumption amounts. Domestic food prices translate these physical aspects into their welfare dimensions for both consumers and producers. Effects upon supporting economic activities, and upon the environment occur at this level as well. Even if climate change affected only a portion of the producers in a market, the range of impacts noted previously would affect all producers through the market system.

The final level shown in Figure 1 is that of the international market. The categories noted at this level are identical to those listed at the domestic market level. However, international trading mechanisms would integrate the single market impacts into the global agricultural economy.

The fact that impacts can be both physical and/or financial is very important. It means that, even in countries where the physical impacts appear at first glance to be totally beneficial (e.g. where higher temperatures increase food production opportunities), the operation of markets may ultimately erode this beneficial position (e.g. through higher prices for goods and services which have to be imported from other areas).

The left-hand side of Figure 1 illustrates that there can be significant linkages between climate change, its various physical and economic effects, and the broader social system. For example, if a change in climate induced a movement from intensive crop production to a rangeland and livestock economy, significant social effects would result. This case would likely lead to less employment in agriculture and its supporting industries. These declining employment opportunities (ceteris paribus) would result in personal and community stress, and probably out-migration from the region. If concerns about adequacy of food supply resulted from the change in climate, another and differing set of social issues could result.

Of course, these physical, economic, and social adaptations would not occur simultaneously. Figure 2 provides a simplistic depiction of the temporal nature of agricultural processes. Here, the system begins *(t=0)* with a set of food inventories and an endowment of agricultural resources. Producers have expectations about future market and climate conditions which dictate the production decisions that are made in period 1. These choices, the resource endowment, and the actual climate of period 1 determine the amount of food production in that period. This production, in conjunction with international market conditions, determines domestic food consumption and price levels.

A key point is that the process identified is continuous in nature. The physical and economic events that occur in period 1 play a key role in determining future actions within the food system. In Figure 2, these carry-over effects are captured in the endowment, producer expectations, and food inventory variables noted for the end of period 1.

Another key point to recognise is that not only are the natural endowment, producer expectation, food inventory and climate variables changing over time, but the variability of these variables is also changing over time. This facet is *not* explicitly depicted in Figure 2, but it is a very important dimension of the impact assessment problem.

Who are the Decision-makers?

To understand the methods most appropriate for decision-making, it is useful to clearly define the types of decision makers who can be expected to find the research results relevant. For AIACCs, the following classification of actors is appropriate:

Figure 2. SCHEMATIC ILLUSTRATING TEMPORAL LINKAGES BETWEEN PRODUCTION PERIODS IN THE AGRICULTURAL SECTOR

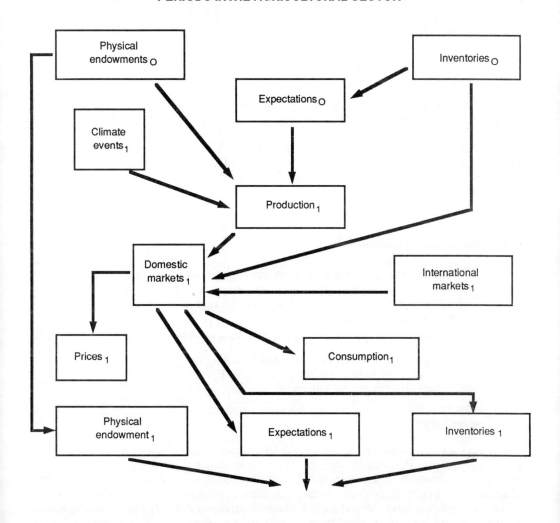

Public Sector

– Political leaders;
– Bureaucrats and institutional managers;
– General populace.

For political leaders, the desirability of new political action, including legislation, is a natural concern. Bureaucrats and institutional managers have a range of non-political factors to consider. (Examples include research initiatives or changes to water management systems.) In addition, bureaucrats are likely to have latitude in the implementation of legislative imperatives. Depending upon each nation's political system, the concerns of the general populace, at a minimum, influence the decisions of political leaders.

Private Sector:

- Agricultural producers;
- Agribusiness managers;
- Consumers.

Agricultural producers and agribusiness managers make long term investments which are based, usually implicitly, on some expectation about the future characteristics of climate. Further, agricultural producers will make short term adaptation decisions in response to a changing climate. Both the nature and degree of these adaptations may be extremely important in determining the ultimate impact of climate change. And finally, consumers are affected by the price and quantity dimensions of climate change's eventual impact on agriculture.

Key Issues Facing Decision-makers

Identifying decision makers allows us to directly consider the types of decision questions of interest. Deriving information which will allow decision-makers to better understand the effect of alternative choices is, of course, the real reason that society should use scarce resources to analyse AIACCs.

In broad terms, three key decision issues dominate society's interest in AIACC:

- Food security (in both its domestic and international dimensions);
- The economics of food consumption and production; and
- Investment in agricultural enterprises and institutions.

Food Security

One of the basic concerns of mankind is food security, an issue with local, national and global dimensions. Potentially, climate change can enhance or diminish a local area's comparative advantage in agriculture. In those societies involved in the international trade of agricultural products, however, local production capabilities must be considered in the context of changing international supply/demand balances. Although food security can be a chronic or long term issue, short term scarcity (due to heightened year-to-year variability of climatic conditions) is also an important social concern.

Food in the Economy

In all societies, food production and/or consumption are major economic activities. Changing local and international supply factors can markedly affect revenues from production and/or costs to consumers. In both cases, profound implications for the general economy are possible. For example, an increased cost structure for food would mean fewer funds available for the purchase of other goods, but may mean higher wealth levels in food-producing areas. Interregional shifts in comparative advantage and associated employment and welfare changes are particularly relevant here.

26

Investment in Agricultural Enterprises and Institutions

Both agricultural producers and managers of agricultural institutions will make investment decisions that can greatly affect the economic and social impact of climate change. Methods to assess climate change impacts, therefore, must reflect the decision environment these managers could face, as well as the range of current and future choices they would consider.

Providing decision-relevant information about the future impacts of climate change on these three broad issues should drive the evaluation of methodological alternatives. It is important to note that these issues, although obviously interlinked, are clearly not of equal social priority. Here, the three issues have been listed in declining order of societal priority, and any methodological tradeoffs that must eventually be made should recognise that ordering.

PREVIOUS APPROACHES TO AIACC

One of the major goals of this paper is to critically review the methodologies employed in prior empirical analyses of AIACC. In doing so, the prior work of Pearce (1989) and Sonka and Lamb (1986) were used as guides to development of the criteria used here. Pearce cited the following major elements to be considered:

- Climate scenarios;
- Uncertainty;
- Specific types of agricultural impacts; and
- Evaluation of impacts.

Building on these general themes, the following set of factors were used:

Climatic Factors and Modelling Considerations:

- Source of climate change parameter estimates;
- Climatic factors considered;
- Timing of climate change;
- Geographic unit of analysis;
- Modelling unit employed;
- Economic model(s) used;
- Motivation of decision-maker;
- Assumptions about changes in non-climate factors;
- Incorporation of uncertainty relative to the extent of climate change;
- Agricultural activities considered.

Effects Measured

- Production effects;
- Shifts in regional comparative advantage;
- Long term environmental impacts;
- Farm profitability;
- National or international food stocks;
- Secondary economic effects.

Table 1. Summary of different case studies on grennhouse effects on agriculture

Paper	Source of Climate Change	Climatic factors Considered	Timing of Climate Change	Area of Study	Model Unit	Economic Model(s)	Motivation of decision-Makers	Assumptions about Changes in Nonclimatic Factors	Decision Making Potential	Uncertainty Climate Change	Agricultural Activities Evaluation
Adams, R.M. et al., (1988)	GCM Output[1]	Temp., Precip., Evapotranspiration CO_2 Fert.	Instant[2]	Continental USA Divided into 9 Regions	Plant[3], Nation[4]	Crop Grow. Econ. Model	Max. Consum., & Prod. Surp.	Future Tech. Region	None	None	Wheat, Corn, Soybean, Cotton
Adams, Richard M., (1989)	GCM Output	Temp., Precip. Evapotranspiration CO_2 Fert.	Instant	64 Geograph. Region of USA	Plant, Nation	Crop Grow. Eco. Simulat.	Max. Econom. Welfare	None	Crop Mix, Mgt. Practice	None	42 Groups & Commodities
Arthur, L. M. et al., (1986)	GCM Output	Temp., Precip. Extreme Events	Instant[5], Extreme	Saskatchewan Manitoba and Alberta, Can.	Plant, Region[6]	Lin. Prog., Input-output	Profit Max.	None	Crop Mix, Mgt. Practice Levels	Alt. Change Levels	Wheat, Oats, Flax, Corn, Hay
Bergthorsson, P. et al., (1987)	GCM Output, Analogue Warm & Cool Climate[7]	Temp., Extreme Events	Instant, Extreme	Iceland	Plant, Region	Regression	Not specif.	Fert. Appl.	Crop Mix, Mgt. Practice Levels	Alt. Change Levels	Hay
Dudek, D. J. (1987)	GCM Output	Temp., CO_2 Effect Evapotranspiration	Instant	17 Westearn States, USA	Plant, Region	Quadratic Program	Max. Economic Welfare	None	Crop Mix, Mgt. Practice	None	Barley, Cotton, Rice, Sorghum, Soybeans, Wheat, Oats
Kane, Sally (1989)	GCM Output Temp., Precip.	Temp., Precip.	Instant	US, Canada, Australia, Argentina, Pakistan, China, Thailand, Brazil, USSR, Northern Europe, Japan, & all others in one group	Inter-national[10]	Partial Equil. Static Intern. Trade Model	Price & Welfare Sensitivities	Alternative	None Demand & Tech.	None	8 Crop, 4 Meat/Livestock, 4 Dairy Products, 2 Protein Meal, 2 Oil Categories

Author	Climate Scenario	Climate Variables	Time	Region	Level	Method	Objective				Crops
Kettunen, L. et al., (1987)	GCM Output, Analogue Warm and Cool Climate	Temp., Precipitation, Extreme Events	Instant, Extreme	Helsinki & Oulu Region of Finland	Plant, Region	Budgeting, Crop Growth, regression	Profit Max.	None	Crop Mix, Mgt. Practice Levels	Alt. Change Levels	Barley, Spring Wheat Oats
Kokoski, M. and V. K. Smith (1987)	GCM Output	Temp., Precip.	Instant	USA	Nation	Computable General Equil. Model	Equil. Welfare Measures	None	None	None	Land, Labor, Capital, Energy, Chemicals, Services, Agriculture Construction Consumer Durables
McKeon, G. M. et al. (1989)	Arbitrary Scenario	Precipitation	Instant	Queensland, Australia	Plant	Threshold Altitude	Not spec.	None	None	None	Maize, Wheat, Sorghum, Sugarcane, Oats
Pitovranov, S. et al., (1987)	Assumed[8], GCM Output, Transient[9] & Analogue Warm & Cool Climate	Temp., Precip., Extreme Events	Instant, Transient, Extreme	Leningrad, Cherdyn, Moscow, USSR	Plant, Region	Crop Growth Econometric, Regional Agr. Planning Model	Central	Technology, Change, Crop Subst.	Crop Mix. Mgt Practice Fert. Distr.	Alt. Change Levels	Winter Rye, Spring Wheat
Rosenzweig, C. (1989)	GCM Output	Temp., Precip. Solar Radiation	Instant	Nebraska, Oklahoma, Kansas & Texas, USA	Plant	Crop Growth	Not specif.	Cultivar	Planting Date	None	Maize, Wheat
Rosenweig, C. (1985)	GCM Output	Temp., Precip.	Instant	Kansas, Oklahoma, Colorado Texas, USA	Plant	Critical Cond. for Wheat Growth	Not specif.	None	None	None	Wheat
Salinger, M. J. (1989)	Arbitrary Scenario	Temp., Precip.	Instant	New Zealand and Temperate Australia	Plant	Threshold Altitude	Not specif.	None	None	None	Pasture Production
Santer, B., (1985)	Arbitrary Scenario	Temp., Precip.	Instant	New Zealand and Temperate Australia	Plant	Statistical & Sim. Model	Not specif.	None	None	None	Wheat
Smit, B. (1987)	GCM Output	Temp., Precip., Evapotranspiration	Instant	Ontario, Canada	Plant, Farm[11] Region	Budgeting	Not specif.	None	Crop Mix, Mgt. Practice Levels	Alt. Change Levels	7 Field Crops

Table 1. **Summary of different case studies on grenhouse effects on agriculture (cont'd)**

Paper	Source of Climate Change	Climatic factors Considered	Timing of Climate Change	Area of Study	Model Unit	Economic Model(s)	Motivation of decision-Makers	Assumptions about Changes in Nonclimatic Factors	Decision Making Potential	Uncertainty Climate Change	Agricultural Activities Evaluation
Smit, B. et al., (1987)	GCM Output	Temp., Precip.	Instant	6 Region in Ontario, Canada	Plant, Region	Crop Growth	Not specif.	None	Crop Mix. Mgt. Practice	None	Grain, Corn, Soybeans, Barley & Hay Forage
Smit, J. B. et al. (1989)	GCM Output	Temp., Precip. CO_2 Fert. Effect	Instant	Great Lakes, Great Plains, California, South-eastern States, USA	Plant, Region	Crop Growth Spatial Equil.	Max. Econ. Welfare	Technology Change	Crop Mix. Mgt. Practice	Alt. Change Levels	Wheat, Corn, Soybeans, Livestock
Williams, G.D.V., et al., (1987)	GCM Output Analogue Past Climate	Temperature, Precipitation Extreme Events	Instant, Extreme	Saskatche-wan, Canada	Plant, Farm, Region	Crop Growth, Farm Level Simulation	Profit Max.	None	Crop Mix. Mgt. Practice	Alt. Change Levels	Spring Wheat & Livestock
Yoshino, m. et al. (1987)	GCM Output Analogue Warm and Cool Climate	Temperature	Instant, Extreme	Hokkaido & Tohoku, Japan	Plant, Region	Crop Growth, Econometric	Not specif.	None	Technical Change	Alt. Change Levels	Rice

1. *GCM Output*: GCM simulation of climate change due to doubling of CO_2.
2. *Instantaneous*: Does not indicate how climate changes over time but assumes equilibrium future climate as a result of doubling of CO_2.
3. *Plant*: Crop response to climate change.
4. *Nation*: Response to climate change at national level.
5. *Extreme*: Anomalously cool and warm climate based on past records.
6. *Region*: Response to climate change at a regional level.
7. *Analogue Cool and Warm Climates*: Warm and cool periods based on past records.
8. *Assumed*: Arbitrary change in climate (temperature ad precipitation) to determine sensitivities.
9. *Transient*: Indicated how climate may change over time. It assumes rate of increase of trace gases.
10. *International*: Response to climate change at international level.
11. *Farm*: Impact assessment at farm level ressource allocation, product mix and profit.

Table 2. **Summary of effects measured**

Document	Production effects	Comparative advantage	Environmental effects	Profitability	Food stocks	Secondary effects
Adams, et al. (1988)	x					
Adams (1989)	x	x	x	x		
Arthur, et al. (1986)	x	x		x		
Bergthorsson (1987)	x					
Dudek (1987)	x			x		
Kane, et al. (1989)	x	x			x	
Kettunen, et al. (1987)	x			x		
Kokoski & Smith (1987)	x					
McKeon, et al.(1989)	x		x			
Pitovranov, et al. (1987)	x		x			
Rosenzweig (1989)	x	x	x			
Rosenzweig (1985)	x	x	x			
Salinger	x		x			
Santer (1985)	x					
Smit (1987)	x					
Smit, et al. (1989)	x	x		x		
Smith, et al. (1989)	x	x	x	x		
Williams, et al. (1987)	x			x	x	x
Yoshino, et al. (1987)	x					x

Tables 1 and 2 describe the results of reviewing 19 empirical case studies in the AIACC area relative to these guidelines. Numerous studies, in addition to those listed here, were reviewed as part of this study and are listed in the bibliography attached. Only those studies that had a strong empirical component were included in Tables 1 and 2.

Climatic Factors and Modelling Considerations

Source of Climate Change

Review of the 19 studies illustrates that output from Global Climate Models models is the dominant source of data relating to climate change. In a few cases, the GCM output is supplemented by analogue data from past climate events. The Salinger (1989) and McKeon et al. (1989), works use arbitrary shifts in climate as indicators of the extent of climate change. Another approach available is that of relying on solicited opinions of experts (National Defence University, not included in Table 1). Use of GCMs is popular because it insures consistency across geographic regions. The coarse spatial resolution of the GMC approach, however, is likely to require the refinement of GCM results by expert opinion, or the use of statistical methods to achieve climate parameter estimates at more economically-relevant geographic scales (Lamb, 1987).

31

Climatic Factors Considered

Temperature is the climate factor considered in all studies, closely followed by precipitation. Failure to include precipitation generally occurred when *1)* that factor was of limited importance to the agricultural sector considered, or *2)* because of the greater uncertainty of the relationship between climate change and precipitation. The potential for a CO_2 fertiliser effect was considered only in a few studies.

Timing of Climate Change

In all but one case, the timing of the climate change hypothesised was assumed to be instantaneous. Except for Pitovranov, *et al.* (1988), analysis of the adjustment from the current climate regime to the specified alternative was not conducted. Extreme events, usually drought, were considered in a number of the analyses reviewed. However, year-to-year variability and the role of extreme events within those dynamics were not evaluated in these cases.

Geographic Unit of Analysis

The dominance of analyses of agriculture in developed nations is apparent in Table 1. Clearly the United States and Canada have been preferred regions for study. Although the size of the agricultural industry in those nations provides partial justification for focusing on them, much needs to be learned about AIACC in Asia, Africa, South America and Oceania. The study by Kane *et al.* (1989), is unique within the group in that its focus is global in nature, emphasising the relationships between agricultural trade and climate change.

Modelling Unit Employed

The vast majority of studies utilise models at the level of the growing plant to estimate climate effects on yields and then incorporate that change in crop potential directly into a more aggregate model to estimate economic effects. The aggregation issue, long a source of error in such processes, is uniformly ignored.

Economic Model(s) Used

Table 1 also illustrates that a range of economic models are used to conduct the aggregate level analyses. These include linear programming, quadratic programming, simulation, and econometric based models. The Kokoski and Smith (1987) effort incorporates a computable general equilibrium model and the study by Kane *et al.* (1989) uses an international trade model. Analysis at the firm level is either ignored, or is conducted using very simplistic techniques.

Motivation of the Decision-Maker

In nearly all cases, individual decision-maker motivations, which are at the root of potential adaptations to climate change, are not considered. At the aggregate level, standard assumptions about behaviour are incorporated except in those cases where the motivation of the decision maker is not specified. Often, this lack of specification reflects a "budgeting" approach to the aggregate analysis.

32

Assumptions about Changes in Non-climatic Factors

Evaluation of the interaction between climate change and key variables such as population growth and changes in resource availability are strikingly absent. In a few cases, the potential for technological change of some type is considered.

Decision-making Potentials

An analysis of potential adaptation by the individual producer is done in a number of cases. However, this adaptation process, which typically is limited to crop mix and a few management practices, is generally accomplished in a very rudimentary fashion.

Incorporation of Uncertainty Relative to the Extent of Climate Change

The existence of major uncertainties about the true nature of future climate change is a factor that is stressed in all the studies reviewed. Despite that concern, a large number of the studies do not include a specific analysis of that uncertainty. In studies that do include this concern, the analysis is limited to fairly simplistic sensitivity modelling of only a few parameters.

Agricultural Activities Considered

The most common type of agricultural activity analysed is that of cereal crop production. In some cases, a range of commodities are considered, although the approach used to indicate crop yield and climate change relationships often is fairly general when multiple crops are considered. A common practice is to base yield change relationships of a group of crops on analysis of climate effects of a single representative crop. Livestock is included in a number of efforts, but that inclusion rarely considers the direct effects of climate change on animal production. Instead, livestock effects are restricted to the demand side of the analysis.

Effects Measured

It is more informative to discuss the types of effects measured as a whole, rather than as a separate section for each of the separate categories of Table 2. Nearly all studies explicitly measure the physical production effects of a change in climate. No study evaluates all six of the potential effects identified. Three studies produce measurements on four of the factors cited.

Comparative advantage, environmental effects and profitability are relatively popular factors to evaluate. It should be noted, however, that even though a single study may have considered a number of factors, that analysis may not have been accomplished in a completely integrated fashion. For example, the environmental effects may have been derived from detailed modelling at the field or watershed area. Profitability, however, may have been assessed using an aggregate model of a regional economy.

A striking result apparent from Table 2 is the paucity of studies that addressed impacts on food stocks. It was argued previously that food security and food sector economics are key driving forces fueling societal interest in this topic. If that is correct, the methods currently used for AIACC do not lead to results that pertain to the basic decision issues that society must address.

33

The previous section of the text described specific characteristics of 19 empirical studies addressing the agricultural impacts of climate change. Although a necessary step toward an understanding of current methodological approaches, that analysis of specifics does not summarise very well the extent to which these studies have addressed the needs of policy-makers who are striving to understand climate change and its potential agricultural effects.

Earlier in this paper, it was suggested that a decision perspective should be used as the driving force for defining an appropriate methodology. Types of decision-makers and the decision questions of likely relevance to them were identified. In summary form, three key decision issues dominate society's interest in AIACC:

- Food security (with both national and international dimensions);
- The economics of food consumption and production; and
- Investment alternatives in agricultural enterprises and institutions.

Providing relevant information about the future impacts of climate change on these three broad issues should drive the evaluation of the appropriateness of any methodological alternatives.

Deficiencies of Current Methodology

Figure 3 illustrates the general types of information needed for decision-makers to effectively respond to the uncertainties surrounding the climate change issue. This schematic summarises the major deficiencies of current methodologies relative to the needs of decision-makers. In Figure 3, major sources of uncertainty are identified as relating to either climatic or non-climatic factors. With respect to AIACC, non-climatic factors can be further subdivided as 1) forces affecting the demand for agricultural production and 2) (non-climatic) factors affecting the agricultural supply potential. Relative to climatic factors, decision-makers are concerned with the impacts that policy actions to lessen the build-up of greenhouse gases will have. Therefore, there are two columns noted under Changed Climate in Figure 3. One is to indicate impacts if no policy responses are instituted, and the other is to indicate that policy measures are employed.

For each of the three sources of uncertainty in Figure 3 (climatic, demand and supply factors), there is a category labelled as current. This entry relates to impact analyses that use current parameter values. Those rows and columns represent analyses providing information that would be useful to validate modelling procedures and to give perspective to decision-makers. Studies that employ only those parameters, however, do *not* directly address the issues faced by decision-makers.

Within the cells of Figure 3, an N indicates the types of analyses conducted now whereas a *D* suggests the type of analyses that are desired to provide decision-relevant information. As indicated in Figure 3, there is a major gap between the information that is available from current methodologies and the information needed for decision-making. The fundamental reason for this gap arises, not from the economic tools utilised, but rather from the underlying perspectives employed. Stated a bit differently, it is very unlikely that any analysis which is not focused on the correct question(s) will provide the most useful answer(s).

Figure 3. SCHEMATIC OF INFORMATION NEEDED TO ADDRESS UNDERLYING UNCERTAINTIES

		CLIMATIC FACTORS		
		CURRENT	CHANGED	
			NO POLICY CHANGE	WITH POLICY CHANGE
DEMAND	CURRENT		N	
	FUTURE	D	D	D
SUPPLY	CURRENT		N	
	FUTURE	D	D	D

NON-CLIMATIC FACTORS

Future Directions

Methodology development must be recognised as being evolutionary in nature. There-fore, rather than suggesting that prior work was methodologically deficient, the discussion surrounding Figure 3 should be viewed as indicating needed future directions. The remain-der of this section will discuss three major thrusts which should underlie future analyses:

- Explicitly addressing changes in non-climatic factors;
- Investigating the dynamic aspects of a changing climate; and
- Broadening the scope of analysis.

Guidelines for implementation of the first two of these thrusts will be provided in the following section of the report.

Explicitly Addressing Changes in Non-climatic Factors

If food security concerns are a major justification for conducting future AIACCs, then future population levels and resource availability are just as important as changes in temperature or precipitation. In addition to population, key factors include the agricultural land base, economic growth, water availability, input costs, and socially-imposed restric-tions on agricultural practices. Accurately predicting all these factors, of course, is an unreachable goal. Considering potential changes in these factors as they interrelate with the AIACC is a reasonable requirement, however.

Further, it must be recognised that each of the reviewed studies has made an implicit assumption about all of these factors, and others. Each of these studies has implicitly assumed that factors would stay at their current levels forever. If there is one assumption that is clearly implausible, it is exactly the one that is used most often.

Significant changes in factors such as climate, population, and resource availability will not go unnoticed. Therefore, failure to explicitly consider decision-maker responses is just as serious as is ignoring the changes in the underlying factors themselves. Indeed, failure to explicitly consider these response functions significantly weakened the credibility of the AIACCs reviewed in this paper. The types of behavioural responses that seem to warrant consideration are:

- Adoption of alternative management practices that producers could employ using existing technologies;
- Changes in food consumption patterns, since consumers respond to differing supply regimes for food; and
- Efforts to create and implement technological improvements which mitigate or exploit alternative climatic regimes.

The process of considering non-climatic factors is interrelated with the incorporation of behavioural adaptations. For example, greater use of irrigation is one currently available management practice that might offset yield reductions due to adverse temperatures, or declines in natural rainfall levels. This response assumes that adequate irrigation water is economically available, a critical assumption. Failure to address uncertainties such as the availability of water for irrigation may send false signals about the resilience of the agricultural system.

Tracing the Path of a Changing Climate

Decision-makers live in a challenging, complex and constantly changing *present*. Analyses that abstract too far from that setting lessen their usefulness, no matter how technically well done. The year 2030 (or any other year 40 to 50 years into the future) may be an excellent reference point for technical and climate reasons. From a decision perspective, particularly when the choice involves action to reduce the emission of greenhouse gases today, economic impact data tied to such a reference point loses meaning. Instead, the dynamics of changing conditions as society moves to that future point in time are of extreme relevance.

The technical feasibility of meaningfully tracing the impacts of a changing climate is a serious question. Our ability to understand and to realistically forecast both climate change and economic response functions oversuch long periods of time is quite limited.

However, it should also be kept in mind that such forecasts would not require the same precision that forecasting quarterly GNP for each of the next five years does. Instead, a broad understanding of the implications of climate change and societal adaptations are the ultimate goal. This (general) perspective may make the process achievable.

Addressing climate change as an evolving process opens tremendous opportunities. One is the explicit analysis of the potential for greater frequency of extreme climate events. Some analysts feel that greater variability may be a feature of a changing climate. If so, that variability may have profound, relatively immediate, implications for decision-makers. When food security and the economics of the global food system are key issues, variability of supply can be as economically relevant as are the average levels of these variables.

Broadening the Scope of Analysis

Analysis of prior studies displays a disappointing consistency of scope. Nearly all considered the impacts of climate change within the framework of cereal crops in developed nations. The economic importance of these activities are significant. But they do not comprise the majority of the world agricultural system. Therefore, there is a need to broaden the scope of analysis, in terms of geographic areas of analysis and agricultural activities included.

Africa, Asia and South America have virtually been ignored, yet from a global food security perspective they are critically important. Similarly the perennial crops, vegetables and livestock, of central importance in many nations, have not been considered. Data availability has been a key determinant driving the framing of analyses to date.

GUIDELINES FOR A MORE ROBUST METHODOLOGY

Earlier in this report, Figures 1 and 2 were used to describe the key features of the agricultural system that are critically linked with the potential for climate change. The major thrusts for improvement of AIACC methodology identified above 5 essentially require a more effective analysis of the spatial and temporal linkages contained in Figures 1 and 2.

As the AIACC methodology evolves to accommodate these needs, broader, more comprehensive, and more resource intensive studies will be required. Just calling for more complex and comprehensive analyses is not, in itself, particularly helpful. There are numerous challenges associated with modelling the complexities of the system depicted in Figures 1 and 2. AIACC, however, is not the only instance where decisions must be made even though the problem setting is "large" and enormous uncertainty about key parameters exists at the time when decisions must be taken. The following discussion of these concerns will draw upon management approaches used when such conditions are present. First, an approach to address the uncertainty problem will be advanced, and then the role of "small" analyses will be discussed.

Using Environmental Scenarios

Within the strategic management literature, the use of environmental scenarios is often advocated to aid decision-makers in understanding the future implications of their current decisions. In this context, the term "environment" includes, but is not limited to, the physical environment, of which climate is a part. Instead, the term environment (as used in the management literature) also includes the social, legal, political and culture dimensions of the problem setting. Although still more of an art than a science, scenario analysis has been used to good effect in assisting decision-making (Wack, 1985).

An essential factor in the successful use of scenario analysis is limiting the number of alternatives with which decision-makers are provided. In general, two or three scenarios are considered. Because there are often a large number of uncertain parameters, the development of *consistent* scenarios should be the goal. One aspect of this desired consistency refers to economic and technical consistency among parameters.

The scenario of major interest is the one that incorporates the most likely parameter values. These "most likely" values refer not just to climate parameters, but to the entire range of variables that relate to AIACC. Reducing a vast range of uncertain parameter values to only two discrete scenarios is a difficult task. Therefore, it has usually been found useful to focus the scenario definitions upon outcomes, rather than on the value of the input parameters. With respect to the climate change issue, one scenario might be defined as the severe food adversity scenario. Parameter values used here would reflect plausible conditions that characterise significant pressures upon agricultural resources. For example, relatively high population growth, loss of land available for agricultural production, restrictions on certain types of inputs, and pessimistic assumptions about water availability would likely characterise this scenario. Conversely, a second scenario might be labelled the "favourable food availability" scenario. In this case, the converse assumptions to those noted previously would be used.

With this approach to scenario analysis, consistency also relates to convergence of assumptions with the theme that characterises the scenario. Clearly, the assumptions adopted must be chosen carefully, and clearly documented for the user. A benefit of this approach is that the theme of the scenario can provide the user with an indication of at least the nature of the assumptions used. Further, the user would not experience the "information overload" problem that arises from the seemingly endless combination of options that can be evaluated when performing sensitivity analysis upon individual parameter values.

Developing consistent, useful scenarios for even a few years into the future is a demanding task. No precise set of equations or rules exists to direct the process. Therefore, use of environmental scenarios to assist in AIACC will be exceedingly challenging, though not impossible. The task is possible because the goal of using environmental scenarios is to assist decision-makers in understanding interrelationships, not to develop predictions.

Much is known about agricultural systems and the economic relationships that are intertwined with that system. Expanding the framework of Figure 3, major demand and supply forces can be identified. For example, key demand components are:

- Population growth;
- Economic activity and personal income levels; and
- Consumer tastes and preferences.

For supply, factors of concern include:

- Resource availability (land, water, and fossil-fuel derived inputs);
- Resource quality (degradation of soils, declining ground water levels);
- Technological change; and
- Societal restrictions on agricultural practices.

Since demand and supply are subdivided into component parts, the process of future speculation becomes more manageable. Prior research results, as well as physical and economic relationships, can be used to provide general perspectives as to likely directions of change.

As noted previously, a "most likely" scenario is commonly defined early in the process. Although not a prediction, development of this specific scenario will attempt to adopt a "moderate" or "middle-of-the-road" policy with respect to parameter estimation, as long as consistent underlying relationships are maintained.

Additional scenarios then can be developed to test key uncertainties. Relative to AIACC, an important scenario would be that of severe food supply adversity. A key step in defining this scenario is identifying the critical characteristics of such a future, if it were to occur. For example, a characteristic of a world suffering from food supply adversity would be high food prices. Here, of course, we are really talking about high prices relative to historic food costs. Declines in global per capita food consumption and in diet quality would be associated with higher prices.

What underlying factors would be linked with such outcomes? Among several logical explanations would be high birth rates in less developed nations; low or minimal productivity gains from new technologies; declines in resource quality (i.e. land and water) in key producing regions; and restrictions on environmentally unacceptable aspects of current technologies. Policy responses of differing types of nations (e.g. developed vs. less developed; food exporting vs. food importing) would be considered as well. Clearly the preceding list is *not* all-inclusive. Hopefully, it does provide a flavour for the needed thought processes.

Two concepts must be remembered. First, the food adversity scenario is defined relative to the most likely scenario. Second, and more importantly, the purpose of the process is to measure the impact of climate change under the food adversity conditions. Therefore, the economic and social modelling results of most interest relate to the differential effects of climate change between the alternative scenarios, not just to the absolute values of the variables that are estimated.

The Role of "Small" Models

Examination of the spatial and temporal linkages of agriculture described in Figures 1 and 2 may give the implication that only global models are relevant for AIACC. The purpose of presenting Figures 1 and 2 was not to suggest that nothing should be done until "perfect" models are available. Rather, Figures 1 and 2 illustrate the framework in which modelling efforts need to be cast to be most effective. There is always the need for modelling of climate effects on only parts of the agricultural system. But the maximum benefits will not be achieved until those studies conduct their analyses within the context of the larger system.

For example, an analysis might consider the responses to climate change at the level of the individual farm unit. That analysis would naturally consider a broad range of management practices as responses to the altered physical environment. Again, scenario analyses could be used to reflect pressures of the larger agricultural system upon the individual producer's choices. For example, the "severe food adversity" scenario would incorporate relatively high real input costs as well as high output prices. Projected yield growth due to technology might be lower than in the most likely case, to reflect environmental concerns of agricultural practices.

Not every study will (or should) attempt to model the entire agricultural system. But individual studies should serve as building blocks upon which societal understanding can be extended.

SUMMARY AND RECOMMENDATIONS

The purpose of this paper is to assist in the development of recommendations aimed at improving the methodology for assessing the socio-economic impacts of climate change on agriculture. In doing so, the analysis *1)* reviewed the methodologies employed in prior empirical studies; and *2)* assessed the adequacy of those approaches in providing decision-relevant information. Several suggestions where than provided for improvements in the basic methodology. This final section summarises the key conclusions of the study, and suggests actions that international agencies might take to aid in the development of improved methodologies for the study of this socially important issue.

A small, but significant body of empirical work exists in the AIACC area. With respect to techniques used (e.g., means adopted to estimate coefficients, climate change assumptions employed, and economic models used), these studies have incorporated appropriate methods. Where methodological problems have arisen in these studies, project resource constraints (typically budgetary ones) are at the root of the problem.

Nevertheless, the results of prior studies have fallen short of the goal of providing the information that decision-makers need to respond economically, effectively, and equitably to the climate change problem. As illustrated in Figure 3, this gap results primarily from the limited perspective employed. Prior studies have almost exclusively assumed an instantaneous shift in climate conditions with no change in non-climate parameters. By doing so, the resulting analyses have had relatively little to say about the potential impacts of climate change on food security and economic activity in the food production and consumption sectors.

It is a complex, resource-intensive task to conduct empirical studies which 1) consider changes in non-climate factors, and 2) strive to incorporate the dynamic implications of a changing climate. Clearly, those researchers who conducted the analyses reviewed in this study recognised the need for considering these perspectives. They faced a serious constraint to doing so, however, because of the lack of a tested protocol and procedure which could be adapted to meet the needs of specific study situations.

Therefore an urgent need exists to develop such protocols. Specifically there is a requirement for:

a) A tested, model protocol for developing a set of environmental scenarios relevant to the question of climate change and agriculture production/consumption activities. One output of such an effort would be parameter estimates for a set of example scenarios for a specific future period. The second, and more important, output would be definition of a process that could be employed in a number of settings and enhanced over time; and

b) Development of processes which would allow analysis of the critically important issues associated with the impacts of a changing climate. Development of this protocol is further complicated because important, unresolved challenges exist for both the atmospheric and socio/economic research communities. However, investigation of AIACC in the context of a dynamic, changing climate is urgently needed to respond to social concerns.

Implementation of both of these recommended initiatives would be particularly appropriate at the international level. Whereas individual nations are, quite naturally, most interested in potential impacts within their boundaries, it it clear that national analyses will be deficient without including the issues of changes in non-climate factors and the dynamics of a changing climate. Further, the processes and procedures appropriate for one nation's analysis are largely applicable for the study of AIACCs in other settings. In effect, the procedures that are needed have some of the features of a public good, warranting investment by an entity that has concerns transcending those of individual nations.

Although the studies reviewed in this report can be viewed as solid first steps in the evolution of a suitable methodology, much more work needs to be done. The two suggestions offered above would be logical next steps. An internationally-coordinated effort could significantly accelerate the process of achieving these next steps.

REFERENCES

ADAMS, R. M., MCCARL, B. A., DUDEK, D. J., and GLYER, J. D. (1988), "Implications of Global Climate Change for Western Agriculture", *Western Journal of Agricultural Economics*, Vol. 13, No. 2:348-356.

ADAMS, R. M. (1989), *Global Climate Change and Agriculture: An Economic Perspective*, Paper presented at AAEA Annual Meeting, Baton Rouge, Louisiana.

ARTHUR, L. M., FIELDS, V. G. and KRAFT, D. F. (1986), *Towards a Socio-Economic Assessment of the Implication of Climate Change for Agriculture in Manitoba and the Prairie Provinces*, Report submitted to Atmospheric Environment Services, Department of Agricultural Economics, University of Manitoba.

BERGTHORSSON, P., BJORNSSON, H., DYRMUNDSSON, O., GUDMUNDSSON, B., HELGADOTTIR, A., and JONMUNDSSON, J. V. (1988), "The Effect of Climatic Variations on Agriculture in Iceland". In: PARRY, M. L., CARTER, T. R.,and KONIJN, N. T. eds, *The Impact of Climatic Variations on Agriculture, Vol. 2: Assessments in Semi-Arid Areas*, Kluwer, Dordecht, The Netherlands.

DECKER, W. L., JONES, V., and ACHUTUNI, R. (1985), "The Impact of CO2-Induced Climate Change on US Agriculture". In WHITE, M.R. (ed.) *Characterisation of Information Requirements of Studies of CO2 Effects: Water Resources Agriculture Fisheries, Forests and Human Health*, US Department of Energy.

DUDEK, D. J.(1987), "Assessing the Implications of Changes in Carbon Dioxide Concentrations and Climate for Agriculture in the United States". In: *Proceedings of the First North American Conference on Preparing for Climate Change*, Climate Institute, 428-450.

HEAL, G. (1989), *Economy and Climate: A Preliminary Framework for Economic Analysis*, Columbia Business School.

KANE, S., REILLY, J., and BUCKLIN, R. (1989), *Implications of the Greenhouse Effect for World Agricultural Commodity Markets*, Paper Presented at the Western Economic Association Conference, Lake Tahoe, California.

KETTUNEN, L., MUKULA, J., POHJONEN, V., TANTANEN, O., and VARJO, U. (1988), "The Effect of Climatic Variation on Agriculture in Finland". In: PARRY, M. L. CARTER, T. R. and KONIJN, N. T., eds, *The Impact of Climatic Variations on Agriculture, Vol. 2: Assessments in Semi-Arid Areas*, Kluwer, Dordecht, The Netherlands.

KOKOSKI, M. F., and KERRY SMITH, V. (1987), "A General Equilibrium Analysis of Partial Equilibrium Welfare Measures: The Case of Climate Change", *American Economic Review*, Vol. 71, No. 3:331-341.

LAMB, P. J. (1987), "On The Development of Regional Climatic Scenarios for Policy-Oriented Climate Impact Assessment", *Bulletin of the American Meteorological Society*, Vol. 68, No. 9:1116-1123.

LIVERMAN, D. M. (1986), "The Response of a Global Food Model to Possible Climate Changes: A Sensitivity Analysis", *Journal of Climatology*, Vol. 6, 355-373.

MCKEON, G. M., HOWDEN, S. M., SILBURN, D. M., CARTER, J. O., CLEWETT, J. F. HAMMER, G. L., JOHNSTON, P. W., LLOYD, P. L., MOTT, J. J., WALKER, B., WESTON, E. J., and WILCICKS, J. R. (1989), "The Effect of Climate on Crop and Pastoral Production in Queensland". In: PEARMAN, G. I. ed., *Greenhouse: Planning for Climate Change*, CSIRO, Melbourne, Australia.

NATIONAL DEFENCE UNIVERSITY (1980), *Crop Yields and Climate Change to the year 2000: Volume I*, Washington, DC.

PARRY, M., and CARTER, T. (1988), *Some Strategies of Response in Agriculture to Changes of Climate*, Prepared for the World Congress, Climate and Development, Congress Centrum, Hamburg, FRG.

PITROVRANOV, S., IAKIMETS, V., KISELEV, V., and SIROTENKO, O. (1988), "The Effects of Climatic Variation on Agriculture in the Subarctic Zone of the USSR". In: PARRY, M. L., CARTER, T. R. and KONIJN, N. T., eds, *The Impact of Climatic Variations on Agriculture, Vol. 2: Assessments in Semi-Arid Areas*, Kluwer, Dordecht, The Netherlands.

ROSENBERG, N. J. (1988), *Global Climate Change Holds Problems and Uncertainties for Agriculture, US Agriculture in a Global Setting: An Agenda for the Future*, National Centre for Food and Agricultural Policy, Resources for the Future.

ROSENBERG, N. J., CROSSON, P., EASTERLING, W. E., FREDRICK, K., and SEDJO, R. (1989), *Policy Options for Adaptation to Climate Change*, Climate Resources Program, Resources for the Future, Washington, DC.

ROSENZWEIG, C. (1989), *Crop Response to Climate Change in the Southern Great Plains: A Simulation Study*, Paper submitted to The Professional Geographer, Department of Geography, Columbia University.

ROZENZWEIG, C. (1985), "Potential CO2-Induced Climate Effects on North American Wheat-Producing Regions", *Climatic Change*, Vol. 7, No. 4:367-389.

SALINGER, M. J. (1989), "Climatic Warming: Impact on the New Zealand Growing Season and Implications for Temperate Australia". In: PEARMAN, G.I., ed., *Greenhouse: Planning for Climate Change*, CSIRO, Melbourne, Australia.

SANTER, B. (1985), "The Use of General Circulation Models in Climate Impact Analysis - A Preliminary Study of the Impacts of a CO2-Induced Climatic Change on West European Agriculture". *Climatic Change*, Vol. 7, No. 1:71-93.

SCHNEIDER, S. H. (1989), "The Greenhouse Effect: Science and Policy", *Science*, Vol. 243:771-781.

SMIT, B. (1987), "Implications of Climate Change for Agriculture in Ontario", *Climate Change Digest*, Environment Canada.

SMIT, B., LUDLOW, L, and BRKLACICH, M. (1988), "Implications of a Global Climatic Warning for Agriculture: A Review and Appraisal", *Journal of Environmental Quality*, Vol. 17, No. 4.

SMIT, B., BRKLACICH, M., STEWART, R. B., MCBRIDE, R., BROWN, M., and BOND, D. (1989), "Sensitivity of Crop Yields and Land Resource Potential to Climate Change in Ontario", Canada, *Climatic Change*, 14:153-174.

SMITH, J. B. and TIRPAK, D. A., eds (1988), "The Potential Effects of Global Climate Change on the United States", *United States EnvironmentalProtection Agency*.

SONKA, S. T. and LAMB, P. J. (1987), "On Climate Change and Economic Analysis", *Climatic Change*, 11:291-311.

WACK, P. (1985), "Scenarios: Uncharted Waters Ahead", *Harvard Business Review*, 63, 72.

WILKS, D. S. (1989), "Estimating the Consequences of CO2-Induced Climatic Change on North American Grain Agriculture Using General Circulation Model Information", *Climatic Change*, 13:19-42.

WILLIAMS, G. D. V., FAUTLEY, R. A., JONES, K. H., STEWART, R. B., andWHEATON, E. E. (1988), "The Effect of Climatic Variations on Agriculture in Saskatchewan, Canada". In: PARRY, M.L. CARTER, T.R. and KONIJN, N.L., eds, *The Impact of Climatic Variations in Agriculture, Vol. 2: Assessments in Semi-Arid Areas*, Kluwer, Dordecht, The Netherlands.

YOSHINA, M., HORIE, T., SEINO, H., TSUJII, H., UCHIJIMA, T., and UCHIJIMA, Z., (1988), "The Effect of Climatic Variations on Agriculture in Japan". In: PARRY, M. L., CARTER, T. R., KONIJN, N. T. eds, *The Impact of Climatic Variations on Agriculture, Vol. 2: Assessments in Semi-Arid Areas*, Kluwer, Dordecht, The Netherlands.

Chapter 3

MODELLING THE ECONOMIC IMPACTS OF GLOBAL CLIMATE CHANGE FOR AGRICULTURE AND TRADE

S.R. Johnson*

INTRODUCTION

Recent evidence of changes in the composition of the atmosphere has sparked an active debate on the possibility of global climate change (Liverman 1986; Rosenberg 1988; Rosenberg, *et al.* 1989; Smith 1988; Smith and Tirpak 1988; Wilks 1989). This has led to an equally active scientific discussion of the possible economic impacts of climate change (Rind *et al.* 1988; Perry 1989). One of the industries most certain to be impacted by global climate change is agriculture (Adams, *et al.* 1988; McQuigg, 1975; Womack *et al.* 1985; Smith, *et al.* 1989; Williams, *et al.* 1987). Crop production patterns and levels, trade in agricultural commodities, cultivation methods, and the very organisation of the food production and distribution systems are all highly dependent on the global climate (Hillel and Rosenzweig 1989).

Questions about the economic impact of climate change for agriculture however, pose difficult analytical and modelling issues. First, the projected changes in global climate may be long term and gradual. Second, the impacts of a change in the global climate would likely be of broad economic scope, affecting output levels, input demands, agricultural policies, agricultural research, trade, and linkages to other sectors of national economies. Third, impacts on the consumer side of the equation for agriculture and food systems could also be significant. When these features of the possible climate change are laid against the fact that economic models are only abstractions or approximations of the systems they represent, the analytical problems for assessments of impacts become evident. How can models only approximating the functioning of the current economic system be applied to study changes that are so fundamental, long term and broad in scope?

The present paper addresses the issue of modelling method choice for studying the impacts of global climate change for agricultural trade. Although the focus of this assessment of modelling approaches will be on agricultural trade, the pervasive nature of potential impacts requires a simultaneous consideration of other aspects of agriculture. The issue

---

* S.R. Johnson is a Professor of Economics and Director of the Centre for Agricultural and Rural Development, Iowa State University, Ames, Iowa, USA.

of impact assessment is first raised in the context of the existing global and other economic modelling systems. These systems in all cases have been developed for other analytical and policy analysis exercises. Thus, the first problem is to identify which questions the existing models are capable of addressing, and how these capabilities can be applied to study the impacts of global climate change for agricultural trade. Second, the more general issue of how alternative modelling systems for studying the impacts of climate change for agriculture and trade in agricultural commodities can be designed and applied is briefly discussed.

The discussion begins with a review of specific modelling issues for linking climate to agriculture and trade in agricultural commodities. This review is not intended to be complete, merely to indicate the complexity of the economic modelling problem, and the importance of identifying prior to the choice of modelling or analytical system, those aspects of the climate change problem to be studied. Criteria for evaluating the capability of modelling systems to assess the impacts of climate change for agriculture an trade are then explored. Currently available alternatives for modelling climate change impacts in agriculture and trade are also reviewed, and a possible modelling approach using existing or extended and elaborated systems is advanced.

SPECIFIC MODELLING ISSUES

The development and adaptation of models for assessing impacts of climate change for agriculture and trade, raises special issues for both production and consumption. And, these issues are complicated by the fact that there would almost certainly be feedback from the production and consumption systems to the climate. Also, since the changes in climate could be long term, the evolution of institutions, policies and agreements governing trade, linkages to non-agricultural sectors, and the use of the natural resource base will also likely accompany the process.

In Figure 1, the broad dimensions of possible climate change impacts are sketched as they could affect agriculture and trade. After briefly commenting on this general representation of the climate change problem, attention will be directed to the production and consumption systems, with emphasis on the former. Most available models for studying climate change are production oriented. In particular, these models link results from global circulation models with simulations of plant growth processes (Rind et al. 1988; Perry 1989). Consumption is only incidentally considered in these systems. Nevertheless, it must be kept in mind that production and consumption are a part of the same system. Figure 1 is intended to suggest possible reactions to global climate change for a single country or nation. Climate change is portrayed as the forcing function in the system. Consumption and production systems are shown as being directly affected, with feedbacks to the climate. Policies and institutions for organising these systems are of course different depending on the nation, and are themselves indirectly responsive to climate change. Trade in agricultural commodities is related to national balances between production and consumption, and in turn influences these balances. Trade policies are shown as being linked to these balances, and to their domestic policy and institutional counterparts. Interactions with other nations or countries are indicated by the second national balances box at the bottom right of Figure 1.

Figure 1. **GENERAL FRAMEWORK FOR STUDYING CLIMATE IMPACTS ON AGRICULTURE AND TRADE**

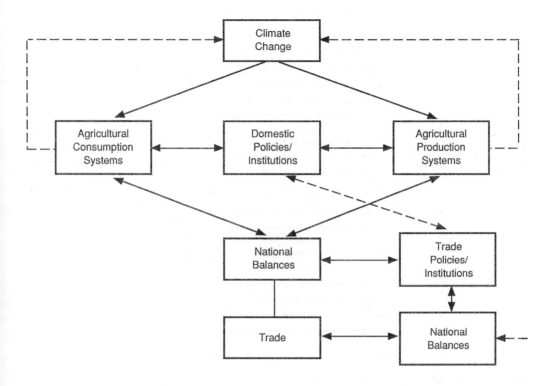

Consumption Systems

Casual observation reveals that consumption systems for food and other agricultural products differ significantly by climate zone. In part, this is because of the local supply of food and other agricultural outputs. However, even if there were no policy or institutional barriers to trade, food supplies would differ due to such things as specialisation in production, processing methods and costs of transportation and distribution. But there is more to observed differences among consumption systems than the food and agricultural products supply. That is, consumption systems as impacted by climate change would likely respond in other ways than just in direct relation to a possibly changed agricultural and food supply.

Activity levels are different among national populations, especially seasonally. Populations have different birth and death rates. Per capita income levels vary widely among nations. Also, there are major differences in non-agricultural employment patterns, due in part to both the climate and the human and natural resource base. These are but a few of the factors that account for the observed differences in consumption systems among

Figure 2. **FACTORS IMPACTING CONSUMPTION SYSTEMS THAT COULD BE INFLUENCED BY CLIMATE CHANGE**

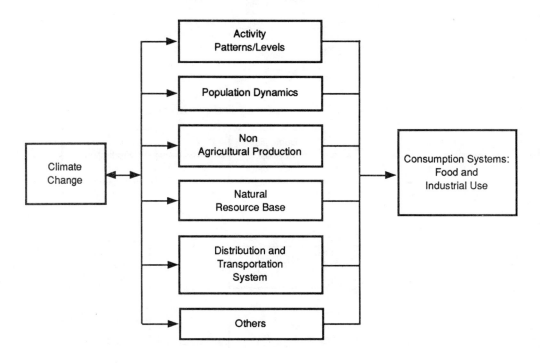

nations. By impacting the determinants of these factors, climate change through consumption response, could in turn have significant implications for adjustments in Figure 1 agricultural production systems and trade. Selected factors impacted by the climate and in turn influencing the consumption systems are illustrated in Figure 2.

The object of this discussion of consumption systems has been to suggest the necessary breadth of systems designed to fully evaluate climate change and agricultural trade (Crosson and Rosenberg, 1989). In short, this brief review of other possible avenues by which climate change may effect agriculture and trade suggests the advisability of adopting a broader research agenda, or alternatively understanding how limited and specialised results from analyses concentrating exclusively on agricultural production systems may be. Not incorporating direct climate impacts on consumption will almost surely result in conclusions that are overly specialised and do not reflect either full climate impacts or the adaptability of production and consumption systems.

Production Systems

The production systems addressed here are for agriculture, and the performance or feature that the evaluation of economic modelling systems will emphasise is trade in agricultural products. The linkages of climate to agricultural production that have received the most attention involve the growth processes for plants (e.g. Rosenberg *et al.* 1988; Smith *et al.* 1989). Animals are, of course, also affected by the climate (Adams, *et al.* 1989; Heal 1989). And, there are both shorter term and longer term impacts. For example, the study of shorter term impacts of global climate change might take the technology for biological production as given at current or trended levels, even though from the history of research and development for agriculture production it is known that technologies are specialised and adapted to particular climatic and growing conditions (Bradford and Johnson 1953; Fischer and Frohberg 1982; Heady 1952; Johnson and Rausser 1977; Ruttan 1989; Simon 1959). A longer term view would recognise that the soils and other components of the ecosystems which support agriculture, the research and technology base, and the institutions governing the organisation of agriculture are all, to an extent, products of past climate patterns (Bouman 1989).

The longer term linkages of global climate change to agriculture production systems and trade are the least understood. But, it is in connection with these longer term linkages that the adaptability of systems will mainly reside. Emphasis on shorter term and more direct effects of climate change in evaluative exercises will almost surely result in overestimation of the impacts on output, input use, international trade and other indicators of performance for production and distribution systems. Thus, these short-term exercises are best seen as pointing to areas of interest for research that are better positioned to reflect the adaptivity of biological and socio-economic systems.

What will be the impact of a gradual temperature increase on plant and animal production processes by location, and how will these biological changes effect the economic organisation of agriculture production and the distribution system? Initially, shorter term assessments of the linkage of climate to agricultural production employed statistical models motivated by growth processes in order to evaluate the impacts of weather on yields and other plant and animal development outcomes (e.g., McQuigg 1975; Bergthorsson *et al.* 1987; Pitovranov *et al.* 1987).

Early studies of weather-plant yield relationships were statistical in nature and used data in aggregated form (McQuigg 1975). In part, these relationships were developed to assist in understanding weather impacts on total crop (and animal) production from particular locations, regions, or nations. Following the more empirical models were statistical specifications which added prior information about phenological or physiological processes (Womack *et al.* 1985). Inclusion of temperature, precipitation and other variables at key points in the plant and animal growth process resulted. For example, there was recognition of the fact that because of the differing water-holding capacities of soils, weather effects would have different time dimensions (Eddy *et al.* 1984).

Modern approaches to the study of weather impacts on plant and animal growth or more generally, on the relationships between climate and agricultural production, utilise "process" models (e.g. Rind *et al.* 1988). These models simulate basic biological processes of energy and water transfer and include significant prior information on how plants and animals grow. Within these models, the interactions between weather and outcomes of the growth process, like grain yield, can be more fully understood. And, these models are now being made more flexible or adaptive to allow application to different climate and cultivation or husbandry conditions, and extended to cover additional plants and animals (Perry 1989).

Summaries of these technical growth processes for plants and animals underlie what are termed "production functions" in economic models. Production functions are simply input-output relationships, and for most economic modelling exercises, have very different time and space scales than are typically applied in plant and animal process models. For

Figure 3. **CLIMATE CHANGE AND AGRICULTURE, LINKAGES
TO PLANT/ANIMAL PRODUCTION**

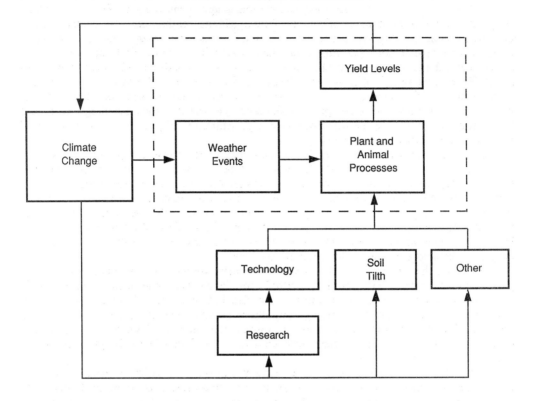

instance, process models have daily time steps and are for a single plant or animal. But, production functions used in economic models are mainly annual and for fields, regions or nations. Clearly then two questions must be addressed if the results of growth process models are to be used in available economic models for analysis of climate changes:

- What are the direct impacts of climate as reflected in animal and plant growth or process models?
- How can these impacts be represented in economic production functions with more aggregated time and space scales?

Figure 3 illustrates selected issues for the first of these questions. For shorter term or more restricted scope analyses, attention is usually within the broken line, on the relationship between weather and plant or animal yield and growth processes. Only two of the other factors conditioning the weather/yield relationships are identified – technology and soil tilth. In more restricted scope analyses, these factors would be assumed unaffected by climate change, and the associated impacts would be assessed, conditional on available information about their current characteristics.

50

Of course, as already mentioned, for longer term or more broadly conceived analyses, soil tilth and the production technology could change or production might be moved to areas in which soils are different (e.g. in carbon content or micro organisms) from those used in developing the process models. The first possibility is illustrated in Figure 3 where climate is depicted as impacting on research. How this relationship is actually played-out represents another difficult analytical problem for building models to assess agricultural production and trade impacts of climate change.

Similar observations suggesting the complexity of the modelling task for studying possible outcomes of climate change can be made for soil tilth, cultivation, or other conditioning factors. The very nature of plant growth under alternative conditions forced by climate change could be different than characterised in process models as they are presently calibrated. And there are feedbacks to climate from changes in production methods and the location of production as indicated by the dotted line in Figure 3.

Figure 4 illustrates the problem of differing time and space scales for linkages between common production or process models, and the production functions used in most economic

Figure 4. TIME AND SPACE SCALES FOR PLANT/ANIMAL PROCESS MODELS AND PRODUCTION FUNCTIONS AS REPRESENTED IN EXISTING ECONOMIC MODELS

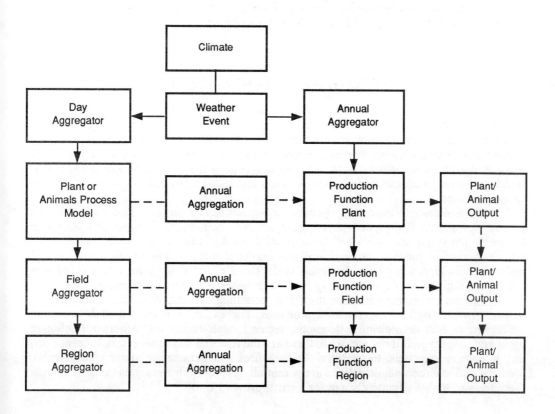

models of agriculture output and trade. The illustration is for a day-time-step plant/animal process model and an annual-time-step economic production function. Also, Figure 4 illustrates aspects of the spatial aggregation problem, represented by progressions from the individual plant to the field and to the region. To further complicate the design of the analytical system for mapping climate to plant and animal growth to agricultural production systems and trade, there may also be interactions between the time-steps and levels of spatial aggregation.

The upshot from this consideration of differences in time and space scales is that experiments or simulations for studying the possible effects of climate change on agriculture production systems and trade must be carefully structured if anything at all is to be learned. When these questions are cascaded with the long-short term and broad-narrow scope issues (see again, Figure 3), designing evaluation systems and assessing impacts of climate change becomes even more difficult. And, this is only one technical aspect, i.e. the production function portion, of the agricultural output and trade assessment problem.

Equally complex, but not as fully explored by past work on climate change are consumption systems, factor mobility and use, institutional design, and other possible aspects of climate change (Kokoski and Smith 1987). In the end, the first round of the "new" global climate change experiments and analyses for agriculture and trade will likely involve only the agricultural production systems (Rosenberg *et al.*, 1989). Even within this limited context however, analysts should carefully attend to the subtleties of linkages between climate, estimates of production response and impacts on agricultural production systems. The associated system design problems are compounded, since the linkages must be introduced into existing models of economic behaviour in order to develop timely public and scientific policy on agricultural production and trade.

ALTERNATIVE ECONOMIC MODELS

Just as there are alternatives for choice of model specification for the linkages between climate and agricultural production systems and trade, there are alternative models for use in evaluating the associated economic impacts. These economic models generally differ in level of aggregation and in the aspect of the economy they are designed to represent. Moreover, these available models have not been specifically designed for study of climate change impacts.

Selected economic modelling systems for agricultural production and trade that are presently available for applied policy analysis and their major linkages are shown in Figure 5. These include individual agent models, market and sector models, multi-sector and multi-market models, national and multinational models, and finally, financial and macro models. Depending upon the aspect of the climate change response to be studied, any one or a combination of these existing modelling systems may be appropriate.

Correspondences between results of the modelling systems if used in combination, however involve difficult aggregation problems. For example, market models represent collections of firm or individual decisions; sector models reflect multi-market (including input and output) equilibria, etc. Also, there are the real and financial sectors in economies, and in economic models, to consider. At both firm and national or multinational levels, financial and macroeconomic policies are potentially important instruments for conditioning the effects of global climate change for agriculture and trade.

Figure 5. **ALTERNATIVE ECONOMIC MODELS FOR CLIMATE IMPACT ASSESSMENT**

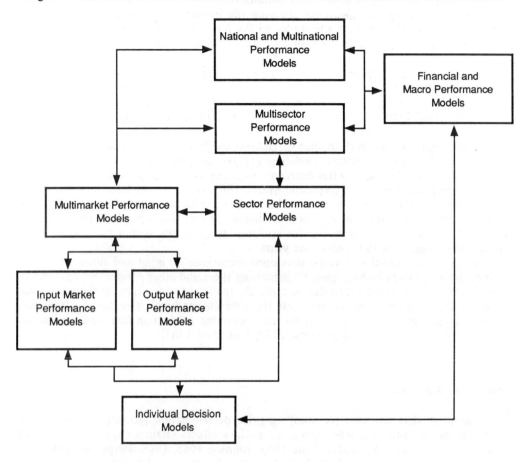

In this section, selected economic models available for evaluating climate change impacts for agricultural production and trade are briefly reviewed. The discussion is designed to indicate the types of agricultural production and trade issues that might be studied for global climate change effects using these alternative constructs. Selected outcomes or performance measures for each model type are also specified. A limited discussion of ways in which policies, interventions or external shocks may be introduced to effect these outcomes is included. As well, the consequences of policies and interventions or external shocks for agricultural production and trade can be explored in the specific models and in "systems" incorporating a number of these models.

Individual Decision Models

Firms and individuals are the primary agents in most economic decision models. This discussion will concentrate on firm-level decisions and, in particular, on farms or firms

53

involved in agricultural production. This follows from the primary focus of the review, to assess available economic models for studying the impacts of global climate change for agricultural production systems and trade. At the farm-level, modelling outputs typical of those that can be generated for assessing impacts of global climate change include:

– Tillage practice choice	– Effects of risk attitudes
– Enterprise selection	– Sequential or within season actions
– Factor use	– Investment levels
– Financial flows	– Government policy impacts

Of course, additional performance variables could be investigated given the alternative firm-level models, initial conditions, policies, and assumptions about global change. And it is at the firm level that sequential decisions involving shorter than annual-time-steps are usually considered (Burt 1964; Cyert and March 1963; Hildreth and Jarrett 1955; Johnson 1981; Steinway 1981; Swanson 1956). That is, the production functions for some of the available firm-level analysis models are for shorter periods than one year. This opens the possibility of using firm-level models for studying dynamic adjustment patterns to global climate change, both within and across years.

Generally, firm-level models are developed conditional on input and output prices and with assumed constant technologies. Endogenising these and other parameters significantly extends the scope of firm-level models as typically applied in agricultural decisions analysis. At present, models that can accommodate these effects use highly structured assumptions on the attitudes of firms toward risk, on the underlying production functions, and on the optimisation criteria (Day and Sparling 1977; Just *et al.* 1983).

Multi-market Models

Market models are used for studying price determination processes, output levels, input use, stocks and economic surplus or welfare effects (Baumas and Meyers, 1979; Chavas and Johnson 1981, 1982; Foote 1953; Johnson 1985, 1988; Judge and Takayama 1973; Thompson 1981; Womack *et al.* 1984). Generally, these models are used to assess the impacts of interventions or policies directed at market performance, or the impacts of external shocks. They can be specified for individual markets or multiples of markets, extending to the national or international levels. Correspondences between market-level and firm or agent-level behaviour require assumptions that are frequently too specialised for applied work.

Generally, specifications of market level behavioural equations in applied systems are frequently motivated by individual or agent behavioural models and equilibrium conditions, and abstract from technical problems of aggregation (Shumway *et al.* 1984; Aradhyula 1989).

The types of responses that can be studied for agricultural production systems to global climate change using available multi-market modelling systems include:

– Prices and stability	– Substitution
– Input use	– International trade
– Output and supply	– Efficiency and welfare
– Policy response	– Dynamics

The dynamics in available market models typically reflect year-to-year or period-to-period persistence. And in multi-market models, these dynamic structures do not usually include the possibility for interplay between markets within periods. Multimarket models have the advantage of permitting analysis of substitution and complementarity in supply and demand. These are features of markets, and the underlying economic and biophysical processes, that would likely be important in buffering, and more generally, in accommodating the direct shocks and indirect effects of global climate change.

Sector Performance Models

Industry or sector models are in fact collections of input and output market models. In addition, they include structures which integrate these components: processing and distribution relationships, linkages among regions, etc. (Cromarty 1959; FAPRI 1989; Halre et al. 1970; Heady and Egbert 1969, 1979; Johnson 1977; Klein and Graham 1985; Ray and Richardson 1978; Tweeten 1975). In modern applications, sector models have been developed using multiple input/ multiple output supply and demand systems and normative representations of economic decision processes (Satheesh 1989).

Issues for global climate change, agricultural production systems and trade that can be studied with available sector level models include:

- Income measures
- Factor use and rewards
- Output levels and values
- Comparative advantage
- Efficiency and welfare

- Technical change
- Interregional trade
- Interregional or intersectoral impacts
- Responses to government policy

Sectors can be specified to include subsectors or regions, and the regions can be differentiated for example, by endowments, technologies, and other features.

National and Multinational Models

National and multinational models are developed for studying aggregated economic policy questions, as well as aggregate effects of shocks generated by such factors as technology and global climate change (Fischer and Frohberg 1982; Johnson 1985; Kuznets 1955). Questions investigated in these models primarily involve international and national performance criteria:

- Income levels
- Factor use, rewards
- Efficiency, comparative advantage and welfare
- Production patterns
- Dynamics

- Output levels
- Multilateral and bilateral trade and mobility
- Technical change
- Government policy responses

It is in these systems that the more general questions of agricultural production systems and trade as well as factor use and mobility and relative input and output prices can be investigated. It is also in these systems that multinational or global impacts of climate change are most appropriately assessed. However, without a clear understanding of the impacts of global climate change at less aggregate levels, these large scale evaluations of multinational effects for agricultural production systems and trade should be interpreted with extreme caution.

Financial and Macro Performance Models

Modelling impacts of global climate change and possible policy interventions on agricultural production systems and trade is also complicated by probable interactions between the real and the financial or macro sectors. Available financial or macro models have been developed to study policy interventions and dynamics (Fair 1980; Johnson 1981; Gardner 1981; Josling 1984; Sargent and Sims 1977; Schuh 1981). Generally, these models include an elaborate flow of funds and government sectors. Government, which can be rationalised, for example, on the basis of market failure in the real sector, can impact both the financial and real sectors (Johnson 1985; Lucas 1976). Macro and financial policies have important impacts on the real sector, and in turn the capacities of agricultural production systems and trade patterns. Issues that can be investigated using available macro or financial policy models include:

- Exchange rates
- Interest rates
- Savings
- Government policy

- Investment
- Dynamics
- Capital transfers
- Financial balances

The host of questions involved with the overlaying of macro and financial policy with policy interventions and external shocks for the real sector stresses the importance of closely focusing analyses of global climate change impacts for agriculture and trade, and of making the appropriate model selection. There is as well he possibility that systems of models may be organised for specialised and more complete analyses.

Government

As previously discussed, government policy influences both financial/macro and real sector performance in national and multinational models. But government is also involved for example, in the organisation and support of research and public information systems. Research and public information systems in turn affect the available technology and the decision processes for economic agents. Due to the propriety of results from private research investment, societies frequently allocate responsibility for at least a part of this investment activity to the public sector. This is especially true for competitive sectors (e.g. agriculture) where the benefits of technical developments accrue to consumers or where there are limited incentives for private investment by producers.

The role of government in research and development is particularly important for broad assessments of global climate change and agriculture. Government policies can alter production and consumption systems for agriculture, fostering adaptation to climate variations and change. In addition, government can influence the allocation of resources to permit improved management of climate change impacts. These improvements in management may include: development of technology and information systems, the organisation of contingency markets for transfer and spreading of risk, institutional change, investments in physical infrastructure and others. The role of government in managing climate change is much more pervasive than would be indicated by the types of policies that can be currently included in existing real sector modelling systems for trade and multinational economic activity. For this reason, it is important to clearly delineate the role of government policy in models used for assessing climate change impacts. Innovative government policy can be a part of the adaptiveness of agricultural economies and aid in accommodating climate changes.

ASSESSMENT OF GLOBAL CLIMATE CHANGE

In the previous sections, climate change outcomes and approaches to evaluation with different modelling systems were reviewed. Also, the interrelationships between the outcomes induced by climate change and other performance and structural characteristics of the models were suggested. For example, in agricultural trade the underlying accompanying outcomes involve: domestic consumption and production systems and their regulation, macro economic and financial conditions and regulations and policies that indirectly effect these systems (e.g. environmental measures).

In this section, specific examples of models currently available for investigating impacts of climate change for agriculture and trade in agricultural commodities are considered. These include multi-market models and multi-sector or multinational models. To give the discussion added substance, specific modelling systems are identified, and their applicability is reviewed. This review includes alternative methods for introducing climate impacts as well as the potential of the models for describing the consequences of the impacts of climate change, once introduced, on long and short-term trade patterns.

CARD/FAPRI Multi-market Commodity Modelling System

This modelling system is described in Figure 6, which shows only those portions that directly involve agricultural trade. The modelling system is designated to include major agricultural commodities used for food, industrial, and animal production. It is dynamic and econometrically estimated from historical data. The countries explicitly modelled are primary exporters and importers of the indicated agricultural commodities. The system is currently being extended to include cotton and livestock and dairy products.

This modelling system was developed to investigate relatively short term impacts of government interventions and exogenous shocks in the international commodity markets. Exogenous shocks could include production and consumption levels reflecting simulated climate outcomes. The external shocks normally considered are from weather or from macro and financial policy. Agricultural policies that have been studied include price stabilisation, trade restrictions, and domestic sector intervention. The opportunities for introducing policy change in this system are directly related to the importance of the included countries in international trade for the identified agricultural commodities. That is, the system is more policy specific for the more important trading countries, e.g., the European Community for wheat and feed grains, Thailand for rice, etc.

57

Figure 6. **CARD/FAPRI WORLD AGRICULTURAL TRADE MODELS**
(Annual Econometric System)

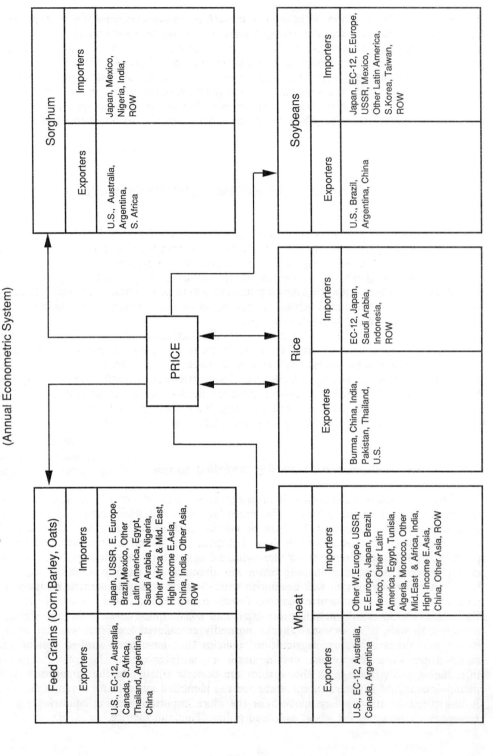

The CARD/FAPRI modelling system is dynamic with a recursive determination mechanism and an allowance for variable biology of crop and animal production over time. The supply and demand functions that underlie the system include lagged producer and consumer responses. These lags are rationalised on the basis of price expectations and biological processes, and of course, reflect assumptions on the constancy of institutions and policies (Chavas and Johnson 1981; Lucas 1976). In most cases, the model specifications are motivated by individual decision theory. But the aggregation conditions required for market level correspondence to the theory for individuals are generally not insured by the specifications. The models should be viewed as approximations of the underlying market systems that concentrate on price determination, output, consumption and trade (Johnson *et al.* 1989).

The CARD/FAPRI modelling system is used for an annual ten year world and U.S. agricultural outlook (FAPRI 1989). For this outlook, policies are specified for the included countries and for the particular commodity markets. As well, macroeconomic and financial conditions are externally imposed. That is, these multi-market models operate conditional on assumed values for the macro or financial factors that directly influence agriculture. There is no feedback mechanism between agriculture and the other sectors of the economy. The economic interlinkages between markets reflect competition for resources and possibilities for substitution in demand or consumption. Although the modelling system is routinely used for ten year projections, its primary economic content is more focused on the shorter term. For the longer term, agricultural policies, population dynamics, and macro economic conditions are likely to change, requiring new solutions for the conditioned system.

Ministerial Trade Mandate Model (MTMM)

This modelling system is maintained and operated at OECD (OECD 1987). It is a multiple-input, multiple-output, market-modelling system, which includes a number of countries and emphasises international trade. The specification is for most traded agricultural commodities. Thus, the commodity coverage is more comprehensive than for the CARD/FAPRI modelling system. A similar modelling system is maintained and operated by the Economic Research Service of the U.S. Department of Agriculture (Roningen, 1986).

Systems like the MTMM are commonly termed "constant elasticity" models. This is because the models are calibrated at reference historical values for endogenous and exogenous variables, and frequently use supply and demand elasticities from other empirical studies, or from a judgmental consensus. The models are static, meaning that time periods and multi-period linkages are not generally included, as is the case for the CARD/FAPRI system. And the models are typically calibrated on the basis of output and factor use levels, as well as trade levels for a reference year. Updating involves changing the elasticities as appropriate, and rolling the calibration forward.

The elasticity models are employed primarily for studying policy impacts. Because of the basic nature of these models, policies can be introduced with a reasonable level of specificity. Types of analyses that have been performed using these modelling systems have included trade policy, domestic output market or commodity policies of specific countries, and input policies. During and leading to the current round of GATT negotiations, for example, a number of these modelling systems have been applied to study the implications of changed trade policy on agricultural trade patterns and agricultural markets in specific countries.

Basic Linked System (BLS)

Basic Linked System (BLS) is a multi-sector general equilibrium model, comprised of national and regional (multi-country) models that are linked in an international framework. The model is for the real (non-financial) sector of the economy (Fischer and Frohberg 1982), and, is an estimated, dynamic, general equilibrium system. Dynamic elements are contained in selected producer decision processes, institutional lags, and physical production processes.

The BLS is very comprehensive, including both agriculture and non-agriculture with a full accounting for world production stocks. The BLS is illustrated in Figures 7 and 8. Because of the multi-sector, multinational nature of this system, the equilibrium process is highly structured. The BLS is in all likelihood the most ambitious international agricultural and trade modelling system developed to date, both in terms of its country and sector coverage, and general equilibrium structure. For this reason, the traded agricultural commodities represented by the system are highly aggregated in order to make the system more manageable. Specifically, there are nine traded agricultural commodities and one non-agricultural commodity in the system. Once again, there is no financial sector in the system.

Figure 7. INFORMATION FLOWS AT THE NATIONAL LEVEL FOR COMPONENTS OF THE BLS

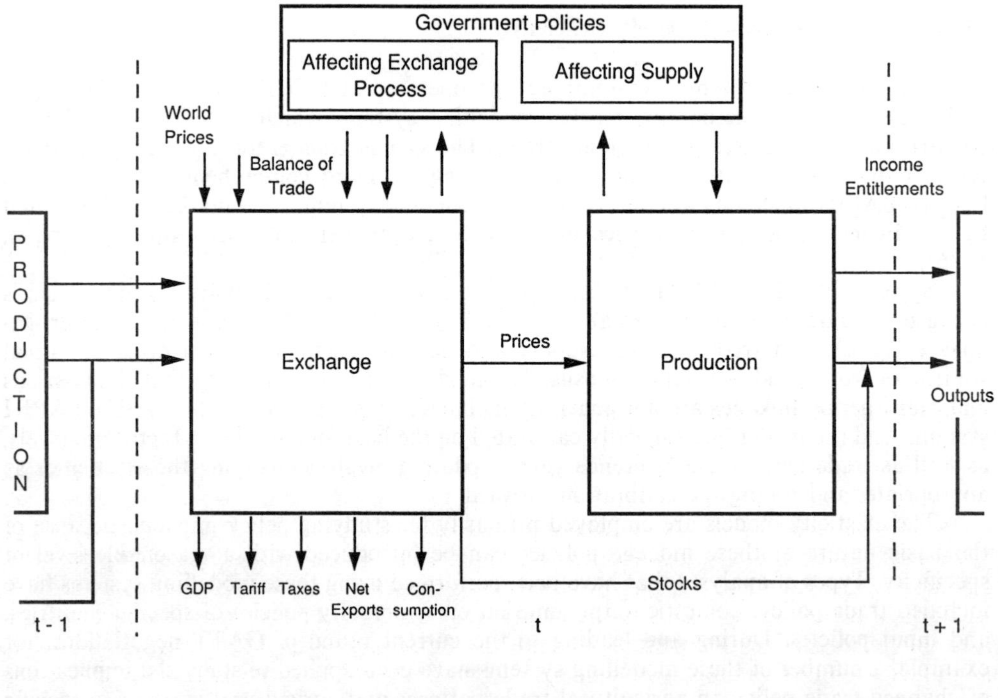

Source: Frohberg and Fischer

60

Figure 8. INTERNATIONAL LINKAGE FOR INDIVIDUAL MODELS IN THE BLS

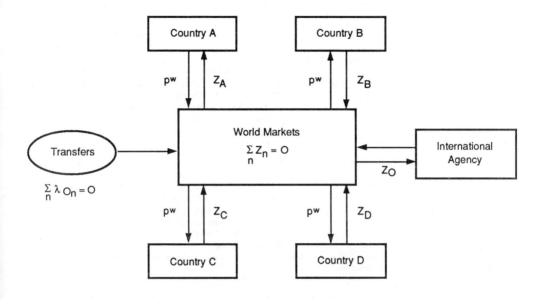

Source: Fischer *et al.*

This is typical of other general equilibrium or sector models, especially if they include a number of countries. One of the reasons for this exclusion is that the micro foundations for the needed macro or financial components are not, at this point, well developed.

Comparisons for the Design of Systems

Tables 1 and 2 summarise country and commodity coverages and the salient structural features of the three models selected for review. The three modelling systems reviewed, of course, have advantages and disadvantages relative to the evaluation of impacts of global climate change for agricultural trade. These concerns relate to dynamic structures, the commodity and country coverage, the level of aggregation, and the policy effects that can be studied. Generally, the BLS is the most highly aggregated relative to the potential for inclusion of specific types of policies. This means that, in the BLS, the policy options studied must be introduced in a stylised fashion. Alternatively, the BLS is a general equilibrium model, and is driven on the basis of more primitive external assumptions, an aspect that is particularly important for longer term assessments.

Table 1. **Country and Commodity coverages in the MTMM, BLS and CARD/FAPRI Models**

Characteristic	MTMM	BLS	CARD/FAPRI
Country Coverage	Canada, Australia, EC, USA, Austria, New Zealand, Japan, Nordic Group, CPE[c], Mediterranean Group and Rest of the World (total of 11 models)	Argentina, Australia, USA, Austria, Brazil, Canada, China, CPE, Egypt, India, Indonesia, Japan, Kenya, Mexico, Nigeria, New Zealand, Pakistan, Thailand, Turkey, EC, & 14 other group models (total of 34 models)	USA, EC-12, Australia, Canada, S. Africa, Thailand, Argentina, China, Japan, USSR, E. Europe, Brazil, India, Egypt, Nigeria, S. Korea, Taiwan, Tunisia, Algeria, & Rest of the World[a]
Commodity Coverage	Wheat, coarse grains, sugar, forage, rice, soybeans, rapeseed, dairy pork, poultry, beef & veal, and sheep meat	Wheat, rice, coarse grains protein, feeds, bovine & ovine meat, dairy, other animal products, other food, nonfood agriculture, (more detailed in some countries; also being updated to 18 commodities)	Wheat, sorghum soybeans, and feed grains (corn, barley, oats)[b]

a) Country coverage changes with commodity.
b) No trade in livestock products. Only the U.S. model has a livestock sector.
c) Centrally Planned Economies.

Table 2. **Major Features of the MTMM, BLS and CARD/FAPRI Models**

Characteristic	MTMM	BLS	CARD/FAPRI
Parameter Calculation:			
Calibration	x		
Estimation		x	x
Time Dimension:			
Dynamic		x	x
Static	x		
Annual	x	x	x
Quarterly			x[a]
General Equilibrium		x	
Partial Equilibrium	x		x
Sample Period	1979-81	1960-76[b]	1965-86
Government Policy:			
Specific	x		x
General		x	
Production/Supply:			
Acreage Analysis		x	x
Output Level	x		

a) The crop sector is annual, while the U.S. livestock sector is quarterly.
b) The BLS is being updated to 1986.

The MTMM and related "elasticity" modelling systems can be specified with high levels of commodity and country detail. But one important problem with these highly detailed specifications is the consistency within the supply side, and between output and input market interactions. Usually, these interactions are specified using limited empirical information. As a consequence, the analytical structures that emerge may have only limited empirical content. But the advantage of these models is that policies can be specifically modelled and studied in substantial detail.

A major limitation of the MTMM for studying agricultural trade and global change is its lack of a dynamic structure. Long term climate change is by nature a dynamic process. The MTMM and related models do not at present include dynamics, and their linkages to the macro and financial sectors are not well developed (due largely to their basic structures). Sophisticated dynamics are difficult to introduce into these modelling systems, since among other factors, the calibration process gives no reasonable basis for estimating the required parameters.

Supporting Models

In addition to the three modelling systems reviewed, several other modelling systems discussed earlier could be included in evaluations of global climate change for agricultural production systems and trade. In particular, farm-level, regional-level, or specific domestic market-level impacts could be studied. These additional models and their associated analyses would provide more information to support the more aggregated analysis from the three main constructs already reviewed. That is, the models could be organised hierarchically, moving from individual behaviour up to more aggregated representations. And even though the focus would be on agricultural trade, there would be an expanded understanding of the underlying economic processes generating the equilibrium trade levels. The correspondences between the modelling systems in such an exercise would not have to be complete. In fact, for common types of policy analyses and for preliminary studies of global climate change, it would not be practical to alter existing systems to allow full model co-ordination, even in cases where it is conceptually feasible.

Key Issues

Climate change will primarily enter these models in terms of production shifts if, as has been implied in the discussion, the emphasis is on the production system. The MTMM model would introduce these shifts as recalibrations. The BLS and CARD/FAPRI systems model production or supply with acreage and yield equations. Thus, for these models, the production adjustments could be entered as a combination of two effects.

A major issue for modelling global climate change, irrespective of the trade model, is how to scale-up from the results of plant growth model simulations to the space and time scales for the economic models. It is likely that these plant growth simulations will be used to convert the simulated climate change or weather series to impacts for yield, acreage or production potential. There are multiple problems with this scaling-up process. Two are highlighted to emphasise the key issues that are involved.

First, plant growth models typically are for points, not for areas. In scaling-up to aggregate national yield levels, how should the estimated responses to the climate data be weighted to reflect soil types, growing area, tillage practices, and the various other factors which would likely change with the climate? The argument here suggests detailing the associated assumptions, so that the results can be properly interpreted.

Second, the output of agricultural commodities estimated in these models presumes an optimising behaviour for producers. Changes in yields will alter optimal input combinations and equilibrium production levels. Simply adjusting existing yields up or down is a gross approximation of this economic response. Acreage allocations in two of the models are also partially yield-determined. These and other vital considerations imply the need for a highly integrated team approach to modelling impacts of climate change for agricultural production and trade on a global scale.

INTEGRATING AVAILABLE MODELS

The theme that emerges from the review of models available for assessing impacts of climate change for agricultural production systems and trade in agricultural commodities is that all have potential for contributing, and that all have strengths and weaknesses relative to the task at hand. The latter is not surprising, since of all the models currently available for assessing climate change impacts for agriculture and trade, none were constructed specifically for this purpose. One possibility is to consider making the assessment with "suites" of models. In addition to the advantages that this integrated approach might have from an economic modelling point of view, there are also attractive features relative to the different types of climate change scenarios likely to be advanced for evaluation.

The climate change scenarios are likely to be two types: dynamic and equilibrium. For the latter, CO_2 is increased by an order of magnitude and climate generators are simulated until they reach an equilibrium. The 'new' climate is then available for analysis. This comparison of climates is, in a number of respects, similar to the use of economic models for comparative static analysis. The dynamic scenarios simulate a build-up of CO_2 and trace temporal adjustments in climate, much like dynamic economic models. Three suites of available models could be considered for evaluating global climate change for agricultural production systems and trade: an aggregate suite, a micro suite, and a country-specific suite. With an integrated approach using suites of models, the emphasis would be on the qualitative assessment of impacts. This would give a richness of results that could be used to better understand the reasons for the estimated aggregate impacts on agriculture and trade in major agricultural economics.

Aggregate Suites

An aggregate suite of models for studying global and climate change could include the three systems reviewed: CARD/FAPRI, MTMM and BLS. Integrating the models would, in fact, be relatively simple. The longer term analysis used for generating a baseline or reference run would employ the BLS. This is because the driving assumptions for the BLS are more primitive, allowing less complicated and plausible projections, or projections with likely lower error levels. As well, alternative policy scenarios for accommodating the climate variations could be more easily communicated with these results.

But the BLS is also limited for analysis of specific policy actions by its high level of commodity aggregation. In contrast, the level of aggregation is a relative strength of the

64

other two modelling systems. At various points in the trajectory of a dynamic global climate change, the CARD/FAPRI and MTMM systems could then be calibrated with the BLS. The CARD/FAPRI systems used to investigate dynamics, explaining in more detail general period to period responses generated by the BLS, and examining sensitivity of the results to more specific policies. Alternatively, different explanations for the dynamic adjustment of trade could be studied using this integrated approach. More specific policy packages, consistent with the general policy settings assumed for the BLS, could also be evaluated.

The MTMM system would provide the advantage of disaggregated commodity and country coverage. This disaggregation could be used to study more specialised policy approaches consistent with the BLS solution. The more detailed policy impacts could be evaluated as a basis for assessing likely directions for policy choice. In general, the application of the suite of models would expand both the policy analysis capacity, and the range of global climate change impacts that could be evaluated. This would be especially the case if different types of climate scenarios were considered. These static and dynamic economic models would then match the set up for the global climate change experiments with the physical analog and process models used to translate these climate changes into productivity and yield responses.

Micro Suites

An alternative modelling system to evaluate impacts of global climate change could include different stages in the aggregation process. Farm level models for specific climatic regions could be evaluated. These farm decision models could be used, for example, to investigate within year adjustments suggested by the climate change. An array of micro decisions at the farm level, as well as the institutions and policies influencing these decisions, could condition the response to climate change in ways that could not be detected in the aggregate models. The emphasis would be to develop improved microfoundations for the aggregate results. The aggregate model specifications, in the sense that they are empirical, reflect climate conditions representative of the past. For responses to alternative climate conditions, models synthesising farm behaviour could be useful. The capacity to synthesise farm behavior in alternative climate conditions in which there is no experience parallels the use that is now being made of the plant growth models in the global climate change analysis. The farm models could then be seen as simply an extended version of the plant growth simulators. The possibility of experimenting with farm or farm simulators in a similar manner to the simulations for the plant growth models is particularly attractive. They could be used to study the link between weather/yield modelling results and production and farm level output (supply) and input (demand) functions. These simulations could eventually be extended to include the financial aspects of farm decisions as well.

Country Suites

These suites would essentially be case studies of direct interest, to provide perspective on the aggregate production and trade results. In these country suites, detailed soil, institutional, infrastructure and other information could be utilised. Also, plant growth models could be modified, for example, to include more appropriate cultivars. And national policies specific to climate change could be considered more directly. Among the policies of interest in the country studies could be those to preserve the status quo. For example, how would policies have to change to maintain trade levels and shares with a global climate change? Subsidisation of irrigation is one example of a policy that could be pursued to maintain agricultural trade and production levels. In short, the country suites would be a particularly attractive arena for investigating the various policy packages that could emerge at the national level as a part of the effort to adapt to climate change.

CONCLUDING OBSERVATIONS

This evaluation of the potential for assessing impacts for agriculture and trade has concentrated on the introduction of global climate change scenarios into commonly available economic models. It has been observed that the nature of the climate changes, and associated changes in the agricultural production system, should be carefully studied before inclusion in standard models for analysis of agricultural trade. The way that climate change and changes in agricultural yields (and acreages) are included in the models can be important in conditioning the results of the assessment exercises.

Alternative available economic models for analysing agriculture and trade were reviewed. The review focused on the interrelationships among the available economic models, and on the types of primary outputs or performance indicators that could be generated. Then, the issue of trade in response to global climate change was more directly considered. Specific modelling systems were evaluated for their potential use in assessing agricultural trade impacts of global climate change. In general, the conclusion was that there were both advantages and disadvantages for all of the models, and that some type of integrated approach would prove most informative.

A natural outcome of this recommendation of an integrated approach was the proposal for consideration of suites of models in evaluations of global climate change impacts for agricultural trade. Possible aggregate, micro, and country-specific modelling suites were briefly described. Each suite would make a different contribution to the evaluation of global climate change, reflecting differing perspectives on the problem of assessing the impacts. In general, the contribution would be to broaden the perspective for investigating policy options, to link farm level decisions and production functions with plant growth simulations, and to provide information on the robustness of the results from the modelling exercises for global climate change.

Another observation concerns the possibility of overquantification. Past analyses of major changes in economic systems have been, more often than not, overquantified. To avoid this problem, the kinds of results that are to be generated, and their audience, need to be specified early in the analysis. For example, is the main question about the relative cost of agricultural production and trade levels among alternative climate regions; the location of agricultural production; the factor use levels; the distribution of agricultural production; the interaction between climate change, policy and trade; or something else? Identifying these questions early and assessing the required modelling outputs, not in a quantitative but in a qualitative sense, could contribute significantly to the value of the results. Also, utilising suites of models would broaden the basis for eventually making quantitative assessments of the impacts of global climate change.

Global climate change is potentially a very important issue for the current agricultural production system, and for trade in agricultural commodities. Currently available models used for agricultural policy evaluation and forecasting can also be used to assess the impacts of global climate change. Because of the likely long term nature of these impacts, existing models which have primitive conditioning assumptions are the most attractive. Results from these exercises with longer term more stylised models could be greatly enhanced by supporting the analyses with alternative specialised modelling systems. This would result in comparative analyses at the same general level of aggregation, but with different time, commodity and country representations. Alternatively, the micro foundations of the aggregate impacts could be investigated with suites of models. Using country suites would have the advantage of providing insights into policy packages that might be adopted in response to climate change. By broadening the scope of the analysis to include alternative economic models, confidence in the estimated impacts can be increased. In short, with comparative analysis, improved guidance can be provided for trade and agricultural policies that may emerge in response to global change.

REFERENCES

ADAMS, R.M., McCARL, B.A., DUDEK, D.J. and GLYER, J.D. (1988). "Implications of Global Climate Change for Western Agriculture", *Western Journal of Agricultural Economics*, Vol. 13, No. 2:348-356.

ADAMS, R.M. (1989). *Global Climate Change and Agriculture: An Economic Perspective.* Paper presented to the Annual Meeting of the AAEA, Baton Rouge, Louisiana.

ARADHYULA, S.V. (1989). *Policy Structure, Output Supply and Input Demand for U.S. Crops.* Unpublished PhD. Thesis, University of Iowa, Ames, Iowa.

BAUMES, H.S. Jr. and MEYERS, W.J. (1979). *The Crops Model: Structural Equations, Definitions, and Selected Impact Multipliers.* USDA, ESCS, NED Staff Report.

BERGTHORSSON, P., BJORNSSON H., DYRMUDSSON O., GUDMUNDSSON B., HELGADOTTIR A. and JONMUNDSSON J.V. (1987). *The Effect of Climatic Variations on Agriculture in Iceland*, IIASA, Laxenburg, Austria.

BOUMAN, A.F. (1989). *The Role of Soils and Land Use in the Greenhouse Effect.* Conference on Soils and the Greenhouse Effect, Washington and The Netherlands.

BRADFORD, L.A. et JOHNSON G.L. (1953). *Farm Management Analysis.* New York: John Wiley & Sons.

BURT, O.R. (1964). "Optimal Resource Use Over Time with an Application to Ground Water". *Management Science* 11:80-93.

CHAVAS, J.P. et JOHNSON, S.R. (1982). "Supply Dynamics: The Case of U.S. Broilers and Turkeys". *Amer. J. of Agr. Econ.* 64:558-64.

CHAVAS, J.P. et JOHNSON, S.R. (1982). "Rational Expectations in Econometric Models", In: *New Directions in Econometric Modelling and Forecasting in U.S. Agriculture*, Gordon C. Rausser (ed.) Elsevier-North Holland.

CROMARTY, W.A. (1959). "An Econometric Model for United States Agriculture". *J. Am. Stat. Assoc.* 54:556-74.

CROSSON, P.R. and ROSENBERG, N.J. (1989). "Strategies for Agriculture". *Scientific American.* Sept. 1989, Vol. 261, 3, pp. 128-135.

CYERT, R. and MARCH, J. (1963). *A Behavioral Theory of the Firm.* Englewood Cliffs, N.J. Prentice-Hall.

DAY, R. and SPARLING, E. (1977). "Optimization Methods in Agricultural and Resource Economics". In: *A Survey of Agricultural Economics Literature,* Minneapolis: Univ. of Minnesota Press.

FAIR, R.C. (1980). "Estimating the Uncertainty of Policy Effects in Nonlinear Models". *Econometrica* 48:1381-91.

FAPRI, *U.S. and World Agricultural Outlook* (1989). University of Missouri-Columbia (CNFAP) et Iowa State University (CARD). FAPRI Staff Report 2-89.

FISCHER, G. and FROHBERG, K. (1982). "The Basic Linked System of the Food and Agriculture Program at IIASA: An Overview of the Structure of National Models". *Mathematical Modelling* 3: 453-66.

FISCHER, G., FROHBERG, K., KEYZER, M.A. et PARIKH, K.S. (1988). *Linked National Models: A Tool for International Food Policy Analysis*. Dordrecht, The Netherlands: Kluwer Academic Publishers.

FOOTE, R.J. (1953). "A Four Equation Model for the Feed-Livestock Economy and Its Endogenous Mechanisms". *J. Farm Econ.* 45:44-61.

GARDNER, B. (1981). "On the Power of Macroeconomics Linkages to Explain Events in Agriculture". *Amer. J. of Agr. Econ.* 63:871-78.

HEADY, E.O. (1952). *Economics of Agricultural Production and Resource Use*. Englewood Cliffs, N.J.: Prentice-Hall.

HEADY, E.O. and EGBERT, A.C. (1969). "Programming Regional Adjustments in Grain Production to Eliminate Surpluses". *J. of Farm Econ.* 41:718-33.

HEAL, G. (1989). *Economy and Climate: A Preliminary Framework for Economic Analysis*, Columbia Business School.

HILDRETH, C. and JARRETT, F.G. (1955). *A Statistical Study of Livestock Production and Marketing*. New York: John Wiley.

HILLEL, D. and ROSENZWEIG C.(1989). *The Green House Effect and Its Implications Regarding Global Agriculture*. Massachusetts Agricultural Experiment Station, Research Bulletin 724.

JOHNSON, S.R. (1977). "Agricultural Sector Models and Their Interface with the General Economy: Discussion". *Amer. J. of Agr. Econ.* 59:133-36.

JOHNSON, S.R., MEYERS, W.H., WOMACK, A. WESTHOFF, P. and DEVADOSS, S., *Documentation for the FAPRI Models* (forthcoming).

JOHNSON, et al. (1981). "Alternative Designs for Policy Models of the Agricultural Sector". In: *Modelling Agriculture for Policy Analysis in the 1980s*. Kansas City: Federal Reserve Bank.

JOHNSON, et al. (1985). "A Critique of Existing Models for Policy Analysis". In: *Agricultural Sector Models for Policy Analysis*, HASSAN, Z.A. and HUFF, H.B. (eds) Ottawa, Canada: Agriculture Canada.

JOHNSON, et al. (1988). "Quantitative Techniques". In: *Agriculture and Rural Development Areas Approaching the Twenty-first Century*. HILDRETH, R.J., LIPTON, K.L. CLAYTON, K.C. and O'CONNOR, C.C. (eds), Iowa State University Press, Ames.

JOHNSON, S.R. and G.C. Rausser (1977). "Systems Analysis and Simulation in Agricultural and Resource Economics". In: Judge, George C. *et al.*, eds., *A Survey of Agricultural Economics Literature, Volume 2*, Minneapolis: University of Minnesota Press.

JOSLING, T.E. (1984). *Markets and Prices: Links Between Agriculture and the General Economy*. Paper presented to the 4th European Congress of Agricultural Economists, Kiel, RFA.

JUDGE, G.G. et TAKAYAMA, T. (1973). *Studies in Economic Planning Over Space and Time*. Amsterdam: North Holland.

JUST, R.E., ZILBERMAN, D. et HOCHMAN, E. (1983). "Estimation of Multicrop Production Functions". *Amer. J. of Agr. Econ.* 65:770-80.

KLEIN, K.K. et GRAHAM, J.D. (1985). "A Canadian Agricultural Regional Programming Model". In: HASSAN, Z.A. and HUFF, H.B. *Agricultural Sector Models for Policy Analysis*. Agriculture Canada, Ottawa.

KOBOSKI, M.F. and SMITH, V.K. (1987). "A General Equilibrium Analysis of Partial Equilibrium Welfare Measures: The Case of Climate Change". *American Economic Review*, Vol. 77, No. 3:331-341.

KUZNETS, G. (1955) "A Survey of Econometric Results in Agriculture: Discussion". *J. Farm Econ.* 37:235-36.

LIVERMAN, D.M. (1986). "The Response of a Global Food Model to Possible Climate Changes: A Sensitivity Analysis", *Journal of Climatology*, Vol. 6, pp. 355-373.

LUCAS, R. (1976). "Econometric Policy Evaluations: A Critique". *J. Monetary Econ.Supplementary Series I*:19-46.

McCARL, B.A. (1982). "Cropping Activities in Agricultural Sector Models: A Methodological Proposal". *Amer. J. of Agr. Econ.* 64:768-70.

McQUIGG, J.D. (1975). *Economic Impacts of Weaker Variability*. Atmospheric Science Department, University of Missouri.

OECD (1987). *Ministerial Trade Mandate Model (MTMM)*, Working Paper, Paris, France.

PERRY, M. (1989). *The Greenhouse Effect and Agriculture in the Future*. The Ninth Asher Winegartin Memorial Lecture, Agriculture House.

PITOVRANOV, S., LAKIMETS, V., KISELEV, V. et SIROTENKO, O. (1987). *Effects of Climatic Variation on Agriculture in the Subarctic Zone of the USSR. International Institute for Applied Systems Analysis*, Laxenburg, Austria.

RAY, D.E. and RICHARDSON, J.W. (1978). *Detailed Description of POLYSIM*. Bulletin Technique T-151, Agronomy Experimental Station, University of Oklahoma, Stillwater, and USDA, Washington, DC.

RIND, D., ROSENZWEIG, A. and ROSENZWEIG, C. (1988). "Modelling the Future: A Joint Venture". *Nature* 334: 483-486.

RONINGEN, V.O. (1986). *A State World Policy Simulation (SWOPSIM) Modelling Framework*. Staff Report AGES860625. Economic Research Service, U.S. Department of Agriculture.

ROSENBERG, N.J. (1988). *Global Climate Change Holds Problems and Uncertainties for Agriculture. US Agriculture in a Global Setting: An Agenda for the Future*, National Centre for Food and Agricultural Policy, Resources for the Future.

ROSENBERG, N.J., CROSSON, P., EASTERLING, W.E., FREDRICK, K. and SEDJO, R. (1989). *Policy Options for Adaptation to Climate Change*, Climate Resources Program, Resources for the Future, Washington, DC.

RUTTAN, V.W. (1989). *United States Foreign Economic Assistance: Food Aid and Agricultural Development*. Paper presented to a workshop of the University of Iowa and the Agency for International Development on "World Food, Trade, Food Security and Aid" Washington, DC.

SARGENT, T.J. and SIMS, C.A. (1977). "Business Cycle Modelling without Pretending to have too Much a Priori Economic Theory". In: C.A. Sims, ed. *New Methods in Business Cycle Research*, Federal Reserve Bank of Minneapolis.

SCHUH, G. E. (1981). "The Foreign Trade Linkages". In: *Modeling Agriculture for Policy Analysis in the 1980s*. Proceedings of a symposium sponsored by the Federal Reserve Bank of Kansas City.

SIMON, H. (1959). "Theories of Decision-Making in Economics and Behavioral Science". *Am. Econ. Rev.* 49:253-83.

SIMON, H. (1979). "Rational Decision-Making in Business Organizations". *Amer. Econ. Rev.* 69:493-513.

SHUMWAY, C.R., POPE, R.D. and NASH, E.K. (1984). "Allocatable Fixed Inputs and Jointness in Agricultural Production: Implications for Economic Modelling". *Amer. J. of Agr. Econ.* 66:72-78.

SMIT, B., LUDLOW, L. BRKLACICH, M. (1988). "Implications of a Global Climatic Warning for Agriculture: A Review and Appraisal", *Journal of Environmental Quality*, Vol. 17, No. 4.

SMIT, B., BRKLACICH, M., STEWART, R.B., McBRIDE, R., BROWN, M. and BOND, D., (1989). "Sensitivity of Crop Yields and Land Resource Potential to Climate Change in Ontario, Canada", *Climate Change*, 14:153-174.

SMITH, J.B. and TIRPAK, D.A. eds (1988). *The Potential Effects of Global Climate Change on the United States*, US Environnemental Protection Agency.

SWANSON, E.R. (1956). "Determining Optimum Size of Business from Production Functions". In: E.O. Heady, G.L. Johnson, and L.S. Hardin (eds) *Research Productivity, Returns to Scale, and Farm Size*, Iowa State Univ. Press.

TAYLOR, B., *et al.*, *AAEA Agricultural Modelling Symposium*. Iowa State University Press.

WILKS, D.S. (1989). "Estimating the Consequences of CO2-Induced Climatic Change on North American Grain Agriculture Using General Circulation Model Information", *Climate Change*, 13:19-42.

WILLIAMS, G.D.V., FAUTLEY, R.A., JONES, K.H., STEWART, R.B. and WHEATON, E.E. (1987). *Estimating Effects of Climatic Change on Agriculture in Saskatchewan, Canada*. IIASA, Laxenburg, Austria.

WOMACK, A.W., YOUNG, R.II. and JOHNSON, S.R. (1985). *Climate Impacts for the U.S. Agricultural Sector*. Paper presented at the Conference for Climate-Economic Impact Assessments: Methods and Applications, Fredericksburg, Virginia.

Chapter 4

IMPACTS OF SEA LEVEL RISE: AN ECONOMIC APPROACH

H.M.A. Jansen, O.J. Kuik C.K., Spiegel*

INTRODUCTION

The build-up of greenhouse gases in the environment, and the changes in the global climate that are expected to result from that build-up, are increasingly being recognised as issues of urgent international concern. Led by the United Nations, the world is now beginning to seriously examine the potential environmental, socio-economic, and policy response impacts of global climate change. In particular, the UNEP/WMO Intergovernmental Panel on Climate Change (IPCC) has recently established three international Working Groups to deal explicitly with each of these broad topics. (This paper was written before the IPCC Working Group Reports were finalised).

Although much of the climate change research effort to date has focused on the environmental changes that might take place, there is a growing awareness of the need to develop an understanding of the socio-economic impacts as well. In effect, it will be important to understand not only how the global climate is changing, but also how these changes impact on our economies and on our societies in general. Without this 'higher order' understanding, it is unlikely that the eventual policy response(s) to climate change will be optimal.

There has been some preliminary work done on assessing socio-economic impacts, but this work is still in the early stages of development. IPCC Working Group 2 recognised early in its mandate that a full socio-economic impact assessment would be hindered by the lack of a clear impact assessment methodology.

This paper consolidates available literature and suggests improvements in the methodological approach to assessing the impacts of Climate Change - induced sea level rise (SLR).

* H.M.A. Jansen is a Professor of Economics at the Institute for Environmental Studies (IES) at Free University, Amsterdam. He has carried out research on a wide range of environmental topics for both national and international organisations.

O.J. Kuik also works at IES as an environmental economist.

C.K. Spiegel studies economics at Hamburg University, and contributed to this paper during a traineeship period at IES.

The impacts of sea level rise include such things as the loss of coastal land; increased risk of flooding; and beach erosion. These impacts will only occur if no adaptive responses are made. With adaptation, damages will be reduced (albeit at certain costs). Considering the assessment problem in a dynamic context, the costs of adaptive responses are thus also part of the damages caused by sea level rise, and should be added to the total value of these impacts. Moreover, adaptive responses can be made by both the private and public sectors, and a distinction should be made between them for impact modelling purposes.

The scope of this paper is limited to adaptive responses to SLR (such as migration or dike construction), and it does not include preventive measures in the sense of reducing emissions of greenhouse gases. Due to differences in the time-frame of the effects of policy measures, there will, in general, not be a direct trade-off between adaptive and preventive measures. This is because emission reduction will not have observable effects for a considerable period of time. In the meantime, adaptive measures will have to be taken anyway.

From the economics' point of view, the sea level rise problem appears to be not essentially different from other environmental problems. This means that no particular shifts in thinking are needed to assess the impacts of SLR. But the long-term character of the SLR phenomenon means that a number of special issues, in particular uncertainty, discounting, and risk, will become more prominent.

The report begins with a summary of the economic literature on SLR. A methodological framework for assessing the impacts of SLR is then presented. Assessing the impacts of a "do nothing" policy scenario then leads to the formulation of alternative policy options. A comparison of these policy options is discussed in the paper. Special problems in this comparison include: the long term nature of SLR; risk; uncertainty; and methods to value impacts. With respect to valuation, it is concluded that SLR is not different from other types of environmental issues. And finally, the paper presents some basic conclusions and recommendations.

LITERATURE REVIEW

Physical Scenarios

The earth's temperature is largely determined by three factors: the sunlight it receives, the sunlight it reflects, and the infrared radiation absorbed by the atmosphere. Without the influence of the atmosphere, incoming visible radiation (in the form of sunlight) and outgoing radiation (in the form of invisible infrared radiation) would balance to result in a certain surface temperature. However, the atmosphere contains gases, such as CO_2 and water vapour, that absorb some of the infrared radiation. These gases are warmed up by the radiation and radiate energy back to the earth's surface, raising its temperature.

The larger the percentage of infrared radiation blocked by the atmosphere, the warmer the earth's surface temperature. This feature of CO2 and certain other gases (methane, nitrous oxide, chlorofluorocarbons) is known as the "greenhouse effect" (Hoffman, Keyes, Titus, 1983). Over the last ten million years, the greenhouse effect has warmed the earth's surface by some 33° centigrade, from an estimated average temperature of −18°C to around +15°C. But for the existence of this background greenhouse effect, the earth would be a cold and lifeless planet (Ettinger et al., 1989).

Figure 1. **MANMADE CONTRIBUTION TO THE GREENHOUSE EFFECT**

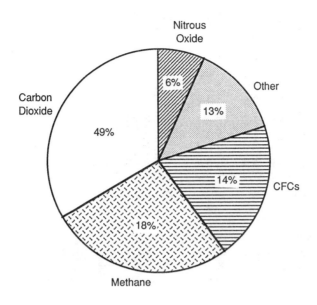

Source: Ruid, 1989.

An increased concentration of man-made trace gases like carbon dioxide (CO_2), methane (CH_4), nitrous oxide (N_2O) and chlorofluorocarbons (CFCs) in the earth's atmosphere will lead to an additional absorption of energy which warms the planet (Rind, 1989). These gases are released in the atmosphere due to many types of activities, but most notably fossil fuel consumption, industrial processes, and deforestation.

If present trends are not counteracted by changes in human practices or by natural processes, a doubling of the concentration of carbon dioxide in the atmosphere from pre-industrial levels could occur over the next 50-100 years (Stokoe, 1987). Figure 1 illustrates the estimated contribution of the various greenhouse gases to global warming (Rind, 1989).

Most estimates of potential warming over the next century concentrate around the 1.5-4.5°C range. As a result of this temperature increase, sea levels could rise as much as one metre in the next century by heating ocean water, which would then expand and cause mountain glaciers and parts of Antarctica and Greenland to melt or slide into the oceans (Titus, Barth, 1984). Although most scientists agree that increased concentrations of greenhouse gases can result in a climate change and, subsequently, in sea level changes, the specific rate and magnitude of these changes is hard to predict.

Various estimates of the rate of temperature rise and sea level rise are illustrated in Table 1.

All studies reviewed for this report are based on an expected doubling of CO_2-concentrations in the atmosphere which will occur in the next 50-100 years. In the same period, the concentrations of other greenhouse gases will increase as well. This might double the

Table 1. **Estimates of temperature rise and sea level rise**

Author	Temperature			Sea level			Explanations
	Year	Rise	Time path	Rise	Time path	Geographical scale	
Bryant		2-4°C (1)				global	(1) Temperature increase towards the poles of 4-8°C
Commission of the European communities	1988	1.5-4.5°C	by 2050	20 cm (2) +16 cm (3) +2-6 cm (4)	next century	Netherlands	(2) Basic trend without greenhouse effect (3) Due to greenhouse effect (4) Above the basic trend in the following centuries
				30-150 cm (5)		global	(5) Over Europe temperature increase could be larger than the world average
Hoffman	1983	1.5-4.5°C (6) 3-9°C		144-217 cm (most likely) 56-345 cm (cannot be ruled out)	by 2100	global (7)	(6) The increasing concentrations of other trace gases could double the warming from CO_2 alone (7) At the Atlantic and Gulf Coast of USA, rise could be 18-25 cm higher than the global average
Marino	1987	2-4°C (8) 1.5-4.5°C	next century (9)	20-140 cm	next century (9)	global	(8) Temp. increase towards the poles of 4-8°C (Hekstra, 1986) (9) (Villach Conference)
Sestini	1987	2-4°C	by 2025	25-30 cm 1-2 m	by 2025 by 2100	global	
Stokoe	1987	4°C 4.7°C	by 2050 by 2050	1 m 1 m	by 2050 by 2050	Newfoundland Labrador	
Sigbjarnarson	1985			15-34 cm 7-18 cm (10) 24 cm (11)	by 2060 by 2060 by 2100	global	(10) (Meier) (11) (Thomas)
Tata Energy Research Inst	1989	0.2-0.5°C	per decade	5-25 cm	per decade (12)		(12) At current trends of emissions
Tirpak	1986	1.5-4.5°C		20-140 cm	next century (13)		(13) Villach Conference
Titus	1986	2-4°C	2020 2060 (14)	30 cm 90-170 cm (110 cm most likely)	by 2025 by 2100		(14) (Hansen et al.) (15) (Thomas)

76

warming effect from CO_2 alone, and could potentially result in a global temperature rise of 3-9°C (Hoffman, 1983).

A great deal of uncertainty surrounds these predictions, because the role of the oceans in the CO_2 build-up process is not completely understood (Crane, Liss, 1983). The most important factor delaying the warming will likely be the oceans' capacity to absorb heat that would otherwise warm the atmosphere. Moreover, estimates of CO_2 uptake by vegetation vary greatly, and the rate of melting-growing of polar and glacier icecaps depends on assumptions made about its calculation (Marino, 1987). Some models also predict cloud cover changes that will provide even more warming, but clouds cannot yet be modelled in a very sophisticated way because the mechanisms are not well understood. Thus, the likely impact of cloud cover changes is still quite uncertain (Rind, 1989).

Many authors accept the following scenario, which was developed at an October 1985 conference at Villach (Austria) "International Assessment of the Role of Carbon Dioxide and other Greenhouse Gases in Climate Variations and Associated Impacts" (World Meteorological Organisation (WMO), United Nations Environment Programme (UNEP), International Council of Scientific Union (ICSU)):

– Temperature increase of 1.5°C leads to a SLR of 20 cm by 2025;
– Temperature increase of 4.5°C leads to a SLR of 140 cm by 2100.

This assumption underlies several recent studies on the impacts of sea level rise (see: Tirpak, 1986; Marino, 1987; Commission of the European Communities, 1988).

Other estimates of future sea level rise differ widely and are difficult to compare, since they focus on different target years (mostly on the years 2025, 2050 and 2100), or on different geographical scales (global, national, regional). Hoffman (1983) indicates a global SLR of 144-217 cm by 2100 "most likely", but in his opinion, a SLR of 56-345 cm by 2100 "cannot be ruled out". Sigbjarnarson (1985) estimates a global SLR of 25 cm by 2100. Thomas (1986) estimates that the irreversible deglaciation of the West Arctic Ice Sheet, which might start to occur in the next century, would raise the sea level by another six metres in the centuries after 2100. Miller (1989) presents a climate model which takes the polar regions into consideration. He comes to the conclusion that sea levels could even fall if the temperature in the Arctic region increases (Die Zeit, 1989).

With respect to the geographical scale, Hoffman (1983) says that on the Atlantic and Gulf Coast of the USA, the sea level rise could be 18-25 cm higher than the global average of 144-217 cm by 2100. Brown (1989) emphasises that actual sea levels will be much higher in some regions than others because of obvious differences (e.g. land elevation), or because of less obvious differences in geological processes (e.g. tectonic uplift or subsidence in coastal areas).

Regional differences in the estimates exist also with regard to the potential temperature increase: Hekstra (1986) estimates that the temperature increase towards the poles will be 4-8 °C above the global average temperature increase of 2-4 °C. The Commission of the European Communities (1988) also estimates that, for Europe, the temperature increase could be larger than the world average.

Overall, the rate of climate change is hard to predict, because scientists are uncertain both about how rapidly heat will be taken up by the oceans and about some climate feedback processes. Generally, scientists assume that current trends in emissions will continue and that climate will change gradually over the next century, but at a much faster pace than historically (Smith and Tirpak, 1988).

There is a fair amount of scientific consensus that sea levels will change as a result of climate change, but current knowledge is inadequate to make a precise prediction of the amount of that rise. Until more reliable climate change and sea level response data becomes available, it will be prudent for policy-makers to use a "high", "medium", and "low" scenario approach.

Economic Impacts

Both an accelerated rate of sea level rise and an absolute increase in mean sea levels would have several impacts on society. These impacts could be either direct (increased flooding, coastal erosion, etc.), or they could be indirect (adaptive responses to the problem by individuals and governments in the form of investment decisions, coastal zone management, approaches, etc.).

The following important types of direct impacts are generally distinguished in the literature:

Effects of Increased Flood Frequencies and/or Permanent Inundation

Jodi L. Jacobson (1989) mentions an unpublished study of the Woods Hole Oceanographic Institute (1988) which shows that the combined effects of sea level rise and subsidence in Bangladesh and Egypt threaten the homes and livelihoods of some 46 million people.

The study developed three scenarios under two estimates of sea level rise: a minimum of 13 cm by 2050 and 28 cm by 2100, and a maximum of 79 cm by 2050 and 217 cm by 2100. The "best case" scenario assumed a minimum rise in global sea level and no additional land subsidence in the delta region. The second scenario assumed a maximum sea level rise and a complete damming of the rivers, causing additional subsidence. The third scenario assumed a maximum sea level rise and an accelerated subsidence caused by excessive groundwater pumping for irrigation and other purposes.

The second scenario results in a projected land loss of 26 per cent and 21 per cent for Bangladesh and Egypt respectively. For Bangladesh, this would mean that about 27 per cent of the population would have to migrate. For Egypt, a figure of 19 per cent is projected. In the worst case scenario, 34 per cent and 26 per cent respectively of land would be lost, causing the relocation of 35 per cent and 24 per cent of the population respectively.

The concept of vulnerability used in the Delft Hydraulics (1988) study encompasses two aspects: 1) the probability and extent of impacts of sea level rise; and 2) the potential of society to prevent or to mitigate these impacts. On the basis of this vulnerability concept (and other considerations), the study selected 10 countries which seem to be particularly vulnerable to sea level rise. They are (in alphabetical order):

- Bangladesh
- Egypt
- Indonesia
- Maldives
- Mozambique
- Pakistan
- Senegal
- Surinam
- Thailand
- The Gambia

(The Maldives are representative of a large number of low-lying island groups in the Indo-Pacific and Caribbean region, and Surinam is representative of countries on the northern coast of South America, which are repositories for silt derived from the Amazon River.)

Potential impact areas in the countries were divided into Primary Impact Areas (PIA), i.e. coastal areas lying below MSL +1.5 m, and Secondary Impact Areas (SIA), lying between MSL +1.5 and MSL +3.0 m. Under the assumption of a 1.5 m sea level rise, the PIAs will be inundated if no adequate defence is available. The SIAs will be affected too, due to assumed population influxes from the PIAs, and due to salt water intrusion and flooding.

Smith and Tirpak assume (1988) that, in the United States, a 1 m rise in sea level would result in the loss of 5 to 10 thousand square miles of land, if no additional protective measures are taken. If the more developed areas will be protected, the loss would still be 4 to 9 thousand square miles. Hekstra (1986) basically rejects such possibilities for the Netherlands. In his view, a sea level rise of up to 50 cm can be accommodated by the existing hydrological infrastructure of the Netherlands. However, larger sea level rises (150 cm) would require fundamental changes and a completely new infrastructure. It has been estimated that a 1 m sea level rise will cause the "overtopping frequency" of existing structures to move from a probability of 1:10,000 to 2:1000 (Den Elzen and Rotmans, 1988). If no precautionary measures were taken, this would mean a serious threat to the safety of the Dutch; about 10 million people would be at risk. For the Netherlands, it is extremely difficult to envisage a "do-nothing" scenario with respect to sea level rise. In fact, existing laws explicitly require the protection of inhabitants against the risk of flooding.

In the Mediterranean countries, a number of low-lying deltas could be flooded. Case-studies of four such deltas (the Ebro Delta in Spain; the Rhone Delta in France; the Po Delta in Italy, including the historical cities of Venice and Ravenna; and the Nile Delta in Egypt), have been prepared for UNEP (Jeftic (1988). The case studies give a rather broad assessment of possible impacts in a mainly qualitative way. More quantitative results are not expected to become available until 1993 (UNEP, 1988).

Park, Armentano and Cloonan (1986) argue that sea level rise would cause wetlands to migrate onto adjacent lowlands. However, because most coastal lowlands have steeper slopes than wetlands, and because many coastlines, (especially those which are commercially developed), will inevitably be protected by dikes and levees, the migration of wetlands inland would be blocked, and a large-scale loss of wetlands can be expected. They estimate the potential loss of wetland at 26-66 per cent in the United States, even if wetland migration were not blocked. Efforts to protect coastal development by building dikes and levees would increase the loss to 50-82 per cent.

Vellinga (1987) points to a "dramatic loss of ecologically valuable wetlands.." in developing countries, because the area directly inland of these wetlands is often used intensively (in Asia, for example, for fish ponds and rice fields). According to Vellinga, local people will not allow inland migration of the wetlands; they will protect their land by building dikes and levees.

In the Netherlands, the consequences of a sea level rise for wetlands were estimated with a simulation model called IMAGE (Integrated Model for the Assessment of the Greenhouse Effect; M. den Elzen and J. Rotmans, 1988). In the Netherlands, there are two important wetland-areas: The Waddensea and the Delta-area (Eastern and Western Scheldt). According to the IMAGE model, the Waddensea-bed level will rise along with sea level, as long as sea level rise does not exceed 1 metre. De Ronde (1987) agrees that it is very probable that a large part of the sea bed of the Waddensea will rise as fast as the water level, but warns that in those places where the bottom level *cannot* keep pace with the sea level rise, the local ecology may change drastically.

There will be losses in the Delta-area. The existing total wetland-area is 800 km², and losses could amount to 60 km², given a 1 metre sea level rise. The Waddensea and the

Delta-area are important feeding and breeding areas for birds, fish and shellfish. Any change in the morphology may decrease the number of species of animals and plants drastically.

In the United Kingdom, it was estimated for the County of Essex that a sea level rise of 0.8 metre could result in a conversion of upper marsh to lower marsh, and a 20 per cent reduction in the area of mud flats. Any rise above 1 metre could lead to a nearly total loss of marsh and a reduction of 30-50 per cent of mud flats (Dept. of Environment, 1988). Selected wetland loss estimates available in the literature are illustrated in Table 2.

Table 2. **Overview of Potential Losses of Wetlands Due to SLR**

Country/Region	SLR	Wetland Loss (percentage)	Source
USA	0.50	17-43	Smith and Tirpak, 1988
USA	1.00	26-66	,,
USA	2.00	29-76	,,
NL (Delta-area)	0.50	1-4	Den Elzen, Rotmans, 1988
NL (Delta-area)	1.00	2.5-7.5	,,
NL (Waddenzee)	0.50	0	,,
NL (Waddenzee)	1.00	0	,,
UK Essex mud flats	0.80	20	Dept. of Env., 1988
UK Essex mud flats	1.00	30-50	,,
UK Essex marshes	1.00	ca. 100	,,

Effects on Coastal Property and Infrastructure

Sea level rise can result in the loss of land above existing water levels, through the process of erosion. Beach erosion can have serious consequences for coastal defences and for tourism. Port facilities, quays, locks, bridges, water intakes and outlets, sewer systems, etc. will have to be adjusted to higher levels. The actual damage caused by a given sea level rise would depend on the economic lifetime of these facilities, and on the annual rate of sea level rise.

An example of potential coastal erosion damage caused by sea level rise is provided by Wilcoxon (1986). Accelerated erosion of Ocean Beach, California, is projected to result in a loss of the recreational beach, damage to a large sewer transport of the city of San Francisco, the Upper Great Highway, and flooding risks for houses near the coast. Wilcoxon estimates that the present value of extra beach nourishment to protect the infrastructure until the year 2100 will amount to about 60 million dollars. Even with such a costly beach nourishment program, a large part of the beach will inevitably be eroded by 2100.

Dunes are an important element of coastal defences in the Netherlands. They protect almost 300 km of the Dutch shoreline. Den Elzen and Rotmans (1988) estimate that a sea level rise of 92 cm by the year 2100 would cause a withdrawal of the shoreline of 29 m. Because of the unacceptable risks this poses for coastal defences, protective measures will have to be taken (beach nourishment), which are projected to cost up to 600 million guilders yearly by the year 2100.

Vellinga (1987) estimates that the protection of beaches along the US Eastern and Gulf Coasts (ca. 5 000 km) will require an investment of between 10 and 100 billion dollars, plus a large amount (not specified) of yearly maintenance. Several other studies on the impacts of sea level rise have estimated the costs of coastal erosion protection (e.g.: Van der Kley, 1987, Barth and Titus, 1984).

A study by Stokoe (1987) on the impacts of sea level rise on coastal infrastructure on the Canadian Atlantic coast, concludes that a major portion of the existing coastal infrastructure (including urban waterfront land, buildings, breakwaters, bridges and causeways, roads and railways) will have to be replaced before the end of their economic lives, if current sea level rise scenarios actually materialise.

Salinisation of Groundwater, Rivers, Bays and Farmland

Salt water intrusion will increase through the landward movement of sea water in rivers, through seepage into surface waters and into ground water aquifers. In the Netherlands, this process would cause damage to agriculture in the coastal provinces, to drinking water supplies, and to existing nature conservation areas.

Although salt water intrusion is often mentioned in the literature on sea level rise, the level of damage potential is seldom quantified.

Coastal and Inland Water Management Regimes

Sea level rise can have serious impacts on water management systems. For example, simple tidal drainage systems will sometimes have to be replaced by pump lift drainage systems. If pump lift drainage already exists (e.g. Italy, Japan, the Netherlands, etc.) the required energy and pumping capacity will often have to be increased [Vellinga (1987)].

Obviously, water management adjustment costs would be largest in countries where the investment in water management systems is already fairly large.

Conversely, improved coastal zone management could reduce the damage caused by sea level rise to some extent. Coastal zone management might include zoning (building) regulations, reallocation of people and industrial facilities from endangered areas, building or strengthening of coastal defence systems, etc. For example, Gibbs (1984) estimated sea level rise damages to the area of Charleston, South Carolina. He concluded that these damages could be halved through anticipatory land-use planning and structural design modifications. An assessment of the possible range of adaptive strategies by coastal zone managers is vital for the final assessment of damages.

Hekstra (1986) mentions the following water management problems for the Netherlands:

- To counteract salt intrusion from beneath the coastal dunes and dikes into the lowlands and into groundwater, the level of rivers, canals and lakes will need to be raised by at least the same amount as the sea level rise;
- Sedimentation of river silt in the coastal harbours is already a problem. Because of sea level rise, sedimentation may occur further inland and in greater amounts;
- The lake IJsselmeer is a large fresh water reservoir in the Netherlands. Major inflows to this lake are provided by rain water on land and from the Rhine through its northern branch, the IJssel. It is separated from the sea (Waddensea) by a large dike. At low tide, surplus water from the IJsselmeer can be drained to the Waddensea through sluices in the dike. Raising the level of the IJsselmeer would require raising all adjacent dikes, including those of the IJssel. But, because the potential

to raise the height of lake IJsselmeer is technically limited, sea level rises larger than 150 cm would require large pumping systems to pump the surplus water into the Waddensea;
- If sea level rises more than 150 cm, the Rhine estuary and the open harbour of Rotterdam would have to be physically closed, and ships would have to pass big sluice complexes. This would require enormous investments, but moreover it could jeopardise the competitive position of Rotterdam harbour, with very significant economic impacts.

For the Netherlands, it is estimated that minimum adjustments to water management systems (accepting lower productivity but maintaining present functions) for a 1m sea level rise would require investments of several billion dollars (Vellinga, 1987). The annual costs of pump lift drainage alone will increase from 12 million guilders to 46 million.

Sea level rise can also damage commercial fisheries, mainly through its potentially negative impacts on wetlands. Wolff (in Wind, 1987) concludes, that, due to a decrease and eventual disappearance of coastal ecosystems, nurseries of fish and shrimp may decrease in size, and that eventually this may be reflected in a decrease of catches offshore.

Similarly, the opportunities for several forms of mariculture, especially shellfish, are likely to decrease. All the above changes would likely affect coastal fishery yields.

One management option for preserving wetlands threatened by sea level rise is suggested by Titus (1986). The greatest threat to wetlands is that their inland migration would be stopped by coastal defence structures on the upland just behind the wetlands. To avoid this, government agencies could buy the property just behind wetlands, but this would, of course, be very expensive. Another option would be for government to include in their permits for coastal zone development the proviso that built property would revert to the state after 100 years if a specified sea level rise occurred. This would offer an incentive for the developer to take a possible sea level rise into account in planning any activity on the property.

A special problem facing coastal zone managers is the presence of hazardous waste sites in coastal areas. The flooding of hazardous waste sites can have serious environmental consequences. In the United States alone, some 1 100 active hazardous waste sites are located within areas that have a probability of being flooded once every hundred years, and in those areas there are possibly as many closed or abandoned sites (Flynn et al. in: Barth and Titus, 1984). Sea level rise will increase the risk of flooding, and thus increase the potential environmental dangers of these sites. Two options are available to mitigate effects: 1) flood protection (not allowing floods to reach the facilities), or 2) floodproofing (flood waters can reach the facilities, but can not cause any damage).

In the face of a rising sea level, coastal zone management must develop strategies to counteract the risks posed by hazardous waste sites in floodplains. Although not found in the literature, a similar remark goes for coastal areas where nuclear power plants are located.

Modelling the Economic Impacts

Most of the existing economic impact modelling literature can be broadly divided into one of three categories:
- Studies that are confined to an assessment of the costs of counteracting measures;
- Studies that go beyond the costs of counteracting measures, and include impacts on

the production and consumption of goods and services for which markets exist; and
- Studies which also attempt to include non-market impacts within their scope.

Studies of Counteracting Measures

There is a relative abundance of studies that assess the engineering costs of counteracting measures, such as strengthening dikes and other coastal infrastructure; adaptation of water management systems; beach nourishment to counteract coastal erosion; etc. The costs of increases in the risks of flood disasters are usually expressed in terms of costs of extra coastal defence structures. Coastal defence is a very important (and perhaps the only feasible) strategy for those coastal areas which are densely populated and highly developed, such as in the North-western part of Europe. Special considerations with regard to the notion of dike construction include:
- Because of the large investments needed, the up-grading of coastal defence systems can have large impacts on the rest of the economy (macro-economic impacts). Also, in developing countries, the dike construction option may not be feasible, due to budget restrictions;
- The construction of dikes to protect uplands can be harmful for coastal ecosystems, and will thus impose ecological costs on society;
- In some cases (e.g. small coral reef islands, such as the Maldives), the building of dikes is not technically feasible.

In the Netherlands, most coastal defence structures (dikes, dunes) are legally required to have an overtopping probability of less then 10^{-4} per year, in order to conform to so-called the "Delta-norm". In practical terms, this means that dikes must be 5m higher than average sea level (NAP+5m). Theoretically, if the sea level rises, these dikes must be raised still further. To keep the coastal defence up to the Delta-norm in the face of rising sea level of 1m in the year 2100, total investments could amount to over 5-6 billion guilders in the next century (Hekstra, 1989). For the United Kingdom, it is estimated that to accommodate a sea level rise of 0.2-1.65m in the year 2050, the improvements of existing sea-defences would cost in the order of 5 to 8 billion pounds [Coker *et al.*,(1989)].

Studies of Market-based Production and Consumption Impacts

Studies in this class range from relatively simple efforts to identify land and capital threatened by sea level rise, to more sophisticated economic growth models, which include changes in sea level rise itself, or in the resulting adaptive response functions. The identification approach is often used as a first indication of potential damage to coastal infrastructure and inundation of unprotected lowlands. Examples can be found in Stokoe (1987) who performed a detailed inventory of coastal infrastructure on the Atlantic coast of Canada. The Delft Hydraulics (1989) study into the vulnerability of low-lying developing countries also identified areas which are likely to be inundated. This study values the potential economic damage by assessing the current economic product (GDP) of these threatened areas. A regional economic growth model is developed by Gibbs (1984), who used it to simulate alternative economic growth paths for the communities of Charleston and Galveston in the USA. In this model, economic growth is influenced by the rate of sea level rise and by the timing and amount of adaptive responses.

The Dutch ISOS (Impacts of Sea Level Rise on Society) model (Wind, 1987) calculates the impacts of sea level rise on society within the framework of a specific scenario

Figure 2. **BASIC STRUCTURE OF ISOS MODEL**

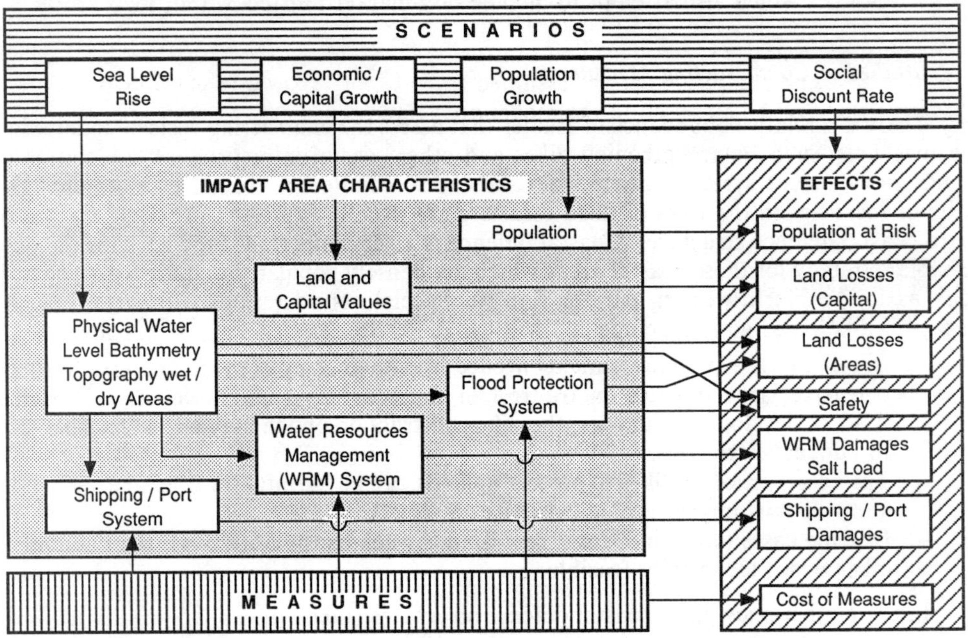

Source: Wind et al., (1987)

consisting of the following elements: rate of sea level rise, economic growth rate, and population growth rate. The social discount rate can be freely imputed by the modeller. The impacts can be counteracted by certain adaptive measures. The model simulates a period of 100 years in discrete time steps of 5 years. The basic structure of this model is illustrated in Figure 2.

The impact *area characteristics* considered include:

- Population;
- Land and capital values;
- Physical characteristics of the area;
- Flood protection system;
- Water resources management (WRM) system;
- Shipping and port system.

The impact *mechanisms* are:

- Land losses;
- Safety against flooding;
- Salt load;
- Damages related to the WRM system and the shipping/ports system.

Land losses depend on the inclination of wet and dry land, and on the presence of a coastal defence system. Safety is measured by the probability of overtopping, which

84

depends on the present probability of flooding plus the sea level rise, minus any increases in height of the flood protection system. The relationship between the probability of overtopping and sea level, is assumed to be log-linear. The salt load can increase both because of seepage (linear relation), and by salinity intrusion into rivers (exponential relation). Damage to WRM and shipping/port are assumed to be of an exponential nature. Adjustment *measures* that can be analysed in the model are related to:

- The flood protection system;
- The WRM system;
- The shipping/port system.

Measures relating to the flood protection system consist of building new dikes or raising existing dikes. Measures relating to the other two systems consist of investments with an assumed declining marginal efficiency. The model takes specific time lags into account to allow for the implementation time required for measures to become effective. For newly built dikes this is 20 years; for raising existing dikes it is 10 years; and for measures relating to WRM and shipping/port systems, the assumed time lag is 5 years.

The *effects* that are calculated by the model are:

- Population at risk;
- Land loss by type of land, in terms of area and capital;
- Safety against flooding, expressed in overtopping probability;
- Total salt load in tons per year;
- Damage to WRM and the shipping/port system;
- Cost of measures.

Table 3 illustrates the results of ISOS calculations for the base scenario, which assume sea level rise of 1.11 m by 2085; population growth of 0.2 per cent per year; and economic/capital growth of 3 per cent per year. The social discount rate used is 0 per cent. No adaptive measures are taken in this scenario. The monetary figures in Table 3 reflect the total impact in the preceding 25 year interval. The other variables reflect the current state of the system at 25 year intervals.

The ISOS model has a clear structure, and can be very useful within limitations. A positive feature of the model is that it tries to assess all major impacts, and that impacts which cannot be easily expressed in monetary terms are shown in their own dimensions. The empirical results in Table 3 are intended only as examples of the working of the model itself, and no great confidence should be attached to the exact outcomes presented. The technical relations within the model can of course be improved upon; new relations can be implemented (e.g. the relation between loss of intertidal land and fish production); and impacts could be assessed better by using a finer regional differentiation.

At the moment, the model is being linked to a Geographical Information System (GIS), which will allow for more detailed geographical impact assessment.

One shortcoming of the ISOS model is the lack of behavioural relations. In other words, the model does not allow for relations between e.g. increased flooding risks and individual investment decisions regarding coastal property, or other secondary economic effects.

One model that *does* try to encompass economic behaviour is provided by Gibbs (1984). This study simulates alternative economic growth paths for the communities of Charleston and Galveston in the USA. Behavioural assumptions in the model relate to private investment decisions and community responses in the face of sea level rise. The model simulates the growth of the regional economic product, which Gibbs calls "Net

Table 3. **ISOS Base Scenario**

Summary Report	1985	2010	2035	2060	2085
Sea level rise (m)	0.01	0.11	0.37	0.81	1.11
Safety A	0.00010	0.00015	0.00036	0.00164	0.00465
Safety B	0.00010	0.00015	0.00036	0.00164	0.00465
Safety C	0.00010	0.00015	0.00036	0.00164	0.00465
Population (10 6)	8.2	8.6	9.1	9.5	10.0
Land capital loss (10 6$)	0.0	0.0	0.0	0.0	0.0
Intertidal cap loss (10 6$)	0.0	3.3	17.3	60.7	82.7
WRM damages (10 6$)	0.0	54.3	254.5	770.7	1 353.9
Shipp/port damages (10 6$)	0.0	28.9	119.7	331.6	557.0
Summ cost measures (10 6$)	0.0	0.0	0.0	0.0	0.0
Total monetary (10 6$)	0.0	86.4	391.5	1 163.0	1 993.6
Total land loss (km 2)	0.00	0.00	0.00	0.00	0.00
Land loss environm. (km 2)	0.00	0.00	0.00	0.00	0.00
Loss intertidal (km 2)	0.00	194.47	678.60	1 520.81	2 094.30
Salt load (ton/year)	215 000	227 268	254 593	302 793	336 043

Present values of:	
Land capital loss	0.0 10 6 $
Intertidal area capital loss	163.9 10 6 $
WRM damages	2 433.4 10 6 $
Shipping/port damages	1 037.2 10 6 $
Summed cost of measures	0.0 10 6 $
Total monetary values	3 634.5 10 6 $

Source: Wind, 1987.

Economic Services (NES)". Net Economic Services of a region are defined as the returns to a set of investments (gross services) minus the costs of these investments. Sea level rise can influence both the returns and cost of the investments, and can thereby alter the set of investments made in the area over time. The model compares the economic performance of an area with and without sea level rise by assessing differences in the present values of the stream of NES over time.

Gibbs argues that models of rational economic behaviour do not describe real behaviour in the face of natural hazards, like floods and earthquakes, very well. He therefore develops another approach. Investment decisions dictate the amounts of funds allocated yearly to reinvestment in existing properties (operation and maintenance), storm damage repair, and new investment. If the perceived rate of damage increases because of sea level rise, a greater proportion of the available investment funds will be necessary to cover these perceived damages.

These "damage coverage" funds must either be taken from reinvestment or new investment, or the total amount of investment must increase. The relation between total investment in response to increasing perceived damages is unclear, but four possible assumptions are examined:

a) Total investment decreases by one-half of the increased perceived damage;
b) No change in total investment;
c) Total investment increases by one-half of the increased perceived damage;
d) Total investment increases by the same amount as the increase in perceived damage.

Gibbs assumes (rather tentatively) that the third assumption seems most plausible. After these investment plans are made by individuals, actual damage can exceed perceived damage. To cover these unexpected damages, new funds are assumed to be added, since all the existing funds would by now already be committed. Thus, because of the initial underestimation of damages, total investments would have to increase, and the relative distribution of investment funds among competing uses would be altered.

Two kinds of individual behaviour are compared by the Gibbs model: one which underestimates future sea level rise (and expected damage) by a fair amount, and one which anticipates sea level rise correctly.

Community responses to sea level rise are not modelled. Instead, two sets of responses (including raising dikes and levees, and the prohibition of investments in certain areas) are assumed. The two sets, one without, and one with, a correct anticipation of future sea level rise, differ by about 20-40 years in the phasing of their implementation.

So basically, three scenarios are developed: the first without sea level rise, the second with sea level rise but without anticipation, and the third with a correctly anticipated sea level rise. The difference between the second and third scenarios indicates the value of anticipating sea level rise, both by individuals, and by community action.

Table 4 presents a few results from applying the model for the community of Charleston, USA. To aggregate the stream of NES over the years 1985-2025, three different discount rates were applied.

From Table 4, it can be seen that the estimated total economic impact of sea level rise (valued at a 3 per cent discount rate) will amount to about $1,065 million in the period 1985-2025. Correctly anticipating sea level rise could reduce this impact by over 60 per cent. Therefore the value of correct anticipation is placed at about $645 million. The table also shows that the discount rate used influences the results considerably, reflecting the fact that sea level rise is a long term phenomenon, whose economic impact will be felt only after some time.

Table 4. **Estimates of Net Economic Services for the Charleston Case Study Area, 1980-2025**

In millions of 1980 dollars

	Real Discount Rate (in percent)		
	3	6	10
Scenario			
A. Trend Scenario	5 395	2 840	1 730
B. High Scenario without Anticipation	4 330	2 570	1 665
C. High Scenario with Anticipation	4 975	2 685	1 675
Results			
Economic Impact (A-B)	1 065	270	65
Value of Anticipation (C-B)	645	115	10

In his analysis, Gibbs assumes that all damages caused by flooding can be avoided. This financial-economic approach, however, does not account for the loss of intangibles (like human lives, property of cultural value, or ecosystems), or irreversible damage that cannot be restored after the fact. In terms of comprehensiveness of coverage, the ISOS model is clearly superior to that of Gibbs. On the other hand, the Gibbs approach deserves some attention for its attempt to incorporate economic behaviour.

Studies Which Include Both Market and Non-market Impacts

Studies in this class recognise that impacts extend beyond what can be readily observed in functioning markets. That is, they explicitly incorporate non-market impacts (where impacts are defined to include both policy and environmental reactions).

The approaches used by this type of study range from simple "what if" types of models to elaborate cost-benefit analyses. In this sense, they are not very different from the market-based class of models described above.

An example of the "what if" approach is provided by the Dutch ISOS model (Wind, 1987). This model estimates impacts using a scenario which contains the following elements: rate of sea level rise; economic growth rate; and population growth rate. The model also explicitly incorporates adaptation possibilities.

Funck (in Wind,1987) identifies three possible strategies to counteract the effects of sea level rise: land-saving (by coastal defence), land-abandoning, or a combination of both. The optimal solution for a region would be a least cost strategy with respect to:

a) construction: either in raising dikes or in reconstruction of residential or production-oriented facilities at new sites, if land is abandoned;

b) change in (real) national income: the real costs of either constructing dikes or of reconstruction should be calculated on an opportunity cost basis. In other words, Funck argues that in the case of idle resources, the expenditure effects of (re)construction on the level of national income should be taken into account;

c) migration: cost of the migration of people and enterprises in case of land-abandoning;

d) loss of land and production, especially agricultural production; and

e) environmental change and social disturbance.

The first four impacts can be expressed in monetary terms. The last impact is expressed in a "societal factor, which is intended to correct or reconsider the relative social importance of the various monetary elements of the evaluation procedure..".

Unfortunately, the paper does not give any practical guidance on how to assess the societal factor, or how it might actually be used in the evaluation itself.

The aim of a recent paper by Nordhaus (1989) is to provide a broad outline of an economic approach to assessing the costs and benefits of alternative approaches to the greenhouse effect. The economic approach consists in the estimation of a greenhouse damage function and an abatement cost function. The damage function describes the cost to society of a changing climate (e.g. damage to crops, recreational amenities, land lost to oceans, etc.). The cost function describes the costs that the economy undergoes to prevent or adapt to the greenhouse effect (e.g. changing from fossil to non-fossil fuels, building dikes, etc.).

Nordhaus estimates marginal damage from greenhouse gases at $3-$37 per ton of CO_2 equivalent in the middle of the next century. Given a rough estimate of the marginal cost function (15 per cent reduction could be achieved for less than $10 per ton CO_2 equivalent, but after that the costs rise sharply), he estimates an optimal reduction of greenhouse gases (in CO_2 equivalents) of 20 per cent to 30 per cent.

Nordhaus estimates damage potential using an EPA report which assumed a sea level rise of 70 cm over the next century. Three types of costs were considered in that study:

- Land loss of 6 000 square miles;
- Protection costs (by levees and dikes) of high-value property;
- Diverse protection of open coasts.

Total capital value is in the order of $100 billion. Nordhaus converts this to the following annual figures in billions of 1981 dollars:

- Land loss $ 0.48 billion
- Protection of sheltered areas $ 0.90 billion
- Protection of open coasts $ 4.80 billion
- Hotels, lodging, recreation   not known
- Total $ 6.18

The annual economic damage due to the doubling of CO_2 concentrations is estimated to be $ 6.67 billion, so damage due to sea level rise would be responsible for 93 per cent of the annual total damage of climate change.

Coker *et al.*, (1989) examine the effects of sea level rise on the current best practice concerning planning of erosion protection schemes. In the past, a static current situation has often been assumed. With a rising sea level, the annual damages will change over time. It is important to have a long term view in project appraisal. Even if the expected life time of a project is 30 years, the project may induce economic activities in the protected zone which will need further protection. They propose using a time horizon of at least 100 years. Because of changes in expected annual damages over time, the timing of projects becomes extremely important. It is necessary to reconsider the optimal design of protection schemes. There may be an advantage to designing works in such a flexible way, so that they can be easily added to at a later stage. Finally, the policy options considered must be expanded from the current "doing nothing" vs. "fixed protection standard", to a variety of options which include (over time and spatial compartments) different combinations of structural and non-structural responses in an integrated way.

Summary

Clearly, an approach that emphasises only the costs of counteracting measures is not sufficient for understanding the full impact of sea level rise. Similarly, the fact that an impact is measurable in a functioning market is not a valid criterion for excluding non-market impacts. The only acceptable approach, therefore, seems to be a comprehensive one. The next section attempts to provide a conceptual framework that is based on this comprehensive approach.

CONCEPTUAL FRAMEWORK FOR ECONOMIC ASSESSMENT OF IMPACTS

A suggested conceptual framework for analysing the economic impacts of SLR is provided in Figure 3. In this framework, "impacts" is broadly defined to include not only

89

Figure 3. FRAMEWORK FOR ECONOMIC APPROACH TO IMPACTS OF SEA LEVEL RISE

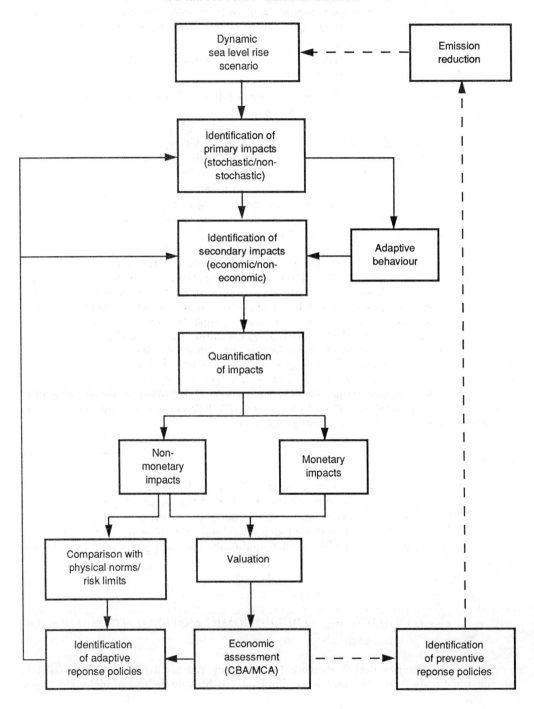

the (residual) damage of SLR, but also the costs of adaptive action. This is because the modelling approach that should be used is a comprehensive. It is also because a preventive or adaptive action that is taken in a given year will affect the level of benefits in subsequent years. In other words, Figure 3 describes a dynamic process.

There are three "feedback loops" in the model, and the first iteration of the model should be interpreted as the "do nothing" scenario. This "do nothing" scenario is the baseline of the assessment. The initial valuation of impacts (at the bottom of the figure) may lead to the formulation of response policies which will, in turn, have new impacts. By reiterating the model, additional policy alternatives can be formulated and assessed.

Another feedback loop pertains to preventive policy measures, that would be taken to reduce emissions of greenhouse gases. Such preventive strategies are not within the scope of this paper. Nevertheless, it should be pointed out that preventive measures will be effective only if they are taken at a large scale. Therefore, a global analysis of potential policies is needed for this part of the model. A full assessment of the global benefits of these policies (i.e. assessment of prevented damages) would be costly and time-consuming. In order to minimise time and costs, it is prudent to first use a "broad-brush" approach, to inventory which areas are most vulnerable with respect to SLR. Guided by the results of this inventory, more detailed assessment should then be carried out. A global policy analysis would also have to include a review of the political feasibility of preventive measures, to be taken in all countries involved (or at least the large majority of them.) Because costs and benefits of global preventive measures will not be spread evenly over all countries, such a study should also investigate the possibility of establishing international cost-sharing principles. In Europe, such studies were conducted with respect to the acidification problem (Klaassen & Jansen, 1989). An important feature of preventive measures is that they will become effective for SLR only in the long term (e.g. only after forty or fifty years).

The third feedback loop pertains to adaptive policy measures (e.g. dike construction). Because this type of policy measure can be taken at a national or local scale, the analysis of impacts can also afford to be made at a smaller scale than the global one. Moreover, the time frame of adaptive measures is different from that of preventive measures. Since policy-makers can sometimes not afford to wait until preventive measures have become effective, preventive measures should not be viewed as strict alternatives to adaptive ones. In other words, because of differences in both the geographical scale and the time frame, there will in general not be a direct trade-off between adaptive and preventive measures; adaptive measures will usually be necessary, even if preventive measures are also taken.

In the following paragraphs each major element of the prepared conceptual framework is discussed in turn.

Dynamic SLR Scenario

The first box in Figure 3 demands a dynamic SLR scenario. This is exogenous input for the framework. From the literature review, it appears that SLR in the next century is projected around a rather wide range (most estimates are in the range of 20-200 cm, with the largest estimate being 345 cm). SLR scenarios can differ by region, and the possible influences of land subsidence also have to be included. The climate change scenario should be a long-term, dynamic one, encompassing at least 50 years.

Given the presently high degree of uncertainty in accurately modelling both climate change and the resulting SLR, it is recommended that a "low", "medium" and "high" scenario be included in the analysis. Timing is another important factor in the response to SLR: how long can policy-makers afford to wait, given the lead-times required to implement policy measures, and given the large uncertainty on the extent of SLR?

Identification of Primary Impacts

In the literature review, the major primary impacts were identified as: effects of permanent inundation of land and wetlands; effects of storm surges and resulting damage to coastal property; salt water intrusion and salinisation of agricultural land, ecosystems and drinking water supplies; and finally, impacts on fisheries.

A well-organised approach to the identification of primary impacts is provided by the ISOS-project (Delft Hydraulics, 1988). This project is not restricted to sea level rise, but addresses the whole problem of climatic change. Figures 4 and 5 depict the relationships between climate change and impacts, as described by ISOS. The ISOS model shows that it is impossible to separate sea level rise from the other effects of the climatic change. For instance, wave climate is influenced both by sea level rise and by other factors resulting from climate change.

Primary impacts can be subdivided into stochastic and non-stochastic components. Stochastic impacts depend on a probability distribution (e.g. storm surges). Given a particular SLR scenario, non-stochastic impacts (such as permanent inundation and salt water intrusion) are fairly predictable, and therefore easier to quantify for input to decision-making processes. However, stochastic impacts (e.g. increased risk of flooding) might well cause the largest damages. A comprehensive study into the risk of flooding was carried out in the Netherlands in 1960 (Delta Commissie, 1960). This study included a statistical analysis to calculate the probability of flooding under various assumptions about the height of dikes. A rise of sea level would cause a shift in the distribution of high tides as shown in Figure 6.

A feedback loop in Figure 3 begins with the choice of adaptive response policies to primary impacts. In a dynamic sense, primary impacts should be viewed as varying with adaptive policies (e.g. changed risk of flooding due to the existence of coastal defence structures). In such cases, the primary impacts of SLR should be viewed as including the costs of these policies.

Adaptive Behaviour/Identification of Secondary Impacts

In this part of the model a distinction is made between adaptive *public* response policy and adaptive *private* response behaviour. Once the primary effects of SLR become known, firms and individuals will likely react on the basis of this information. An example is given in Gibbs (1984), where investors explicitly anticipate primary impacts. This anticipation leads to other forms of private adaptive behaviour, which, in turn, causes the secondary impacts of SLR to be modified. The secondary impacts themselves include such things as disrupted traffic patterns or income flows; unemployment resulting from flooding; migration of people to less vulnerable areas; etc. Clearly, in order to properly evaluate secondary impacts, models of private sector adaptive behaviour will be required. Secondary impacts can also be "secondary" in terms of geographical space (i.e. location of the impacts), or in terms of time (e.g. intergenerational impacts).

Figure 4. GENERAL SUBSYSTEM OF IMPACTS. (ISOS MODEL)

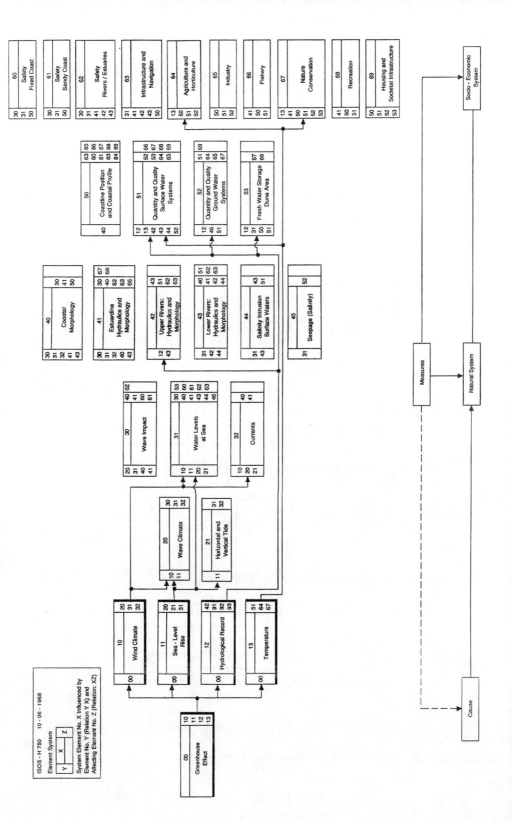

Figure 5. SUBSYSTEM OF SEAS, COASTAL SEAS AND ESTUARIES (ISOS MODEL)

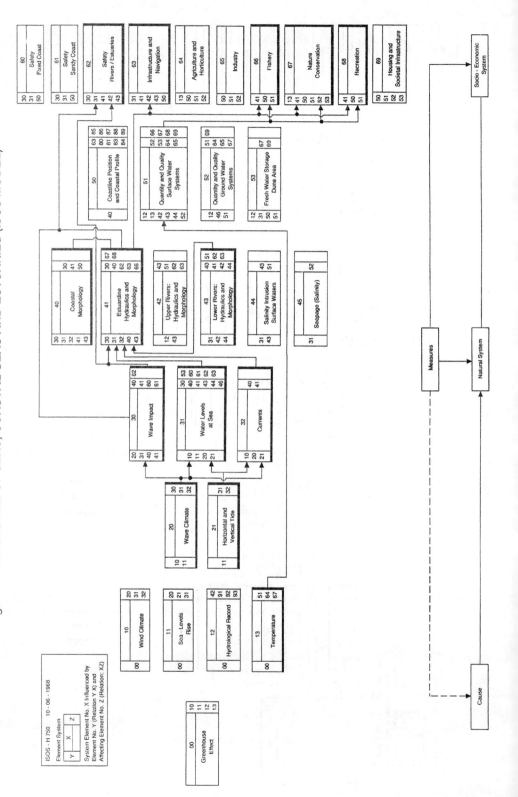

Figure 6. SHIFT IN PROBABILITY DISTRIBUTION OF HIGH TIDES, DUE TO SEA LEVEL RISE

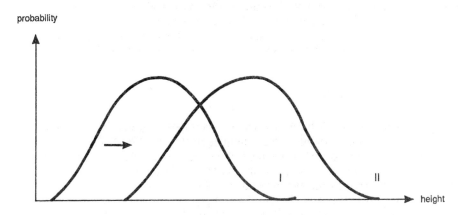

Quantification of Impacts

In view of the long-term nature of SLR, all attempts to quantify impacts will be speculative and subject to great uncertainty. Apart from physical impacts, SLR will also lead to economic impacts, in the sense of changes in economic variables such as GNP, employment, balance of payments, etc. To quantify economic impacts, various economic models (input-output analysis, macro-economic models) can be used to assess such things as the economic consequences of diminished fish catches; flooding on an important harbour; of diminished tourism; or the macro-economic consequences of a coastal defence programme.

Although it will always be speculative to quantify future damages, even data on near-term damages will not always be readily available. Data availability differs strongly between countries, especially with respect to the altitudes of vulnerable areas and the location of flood-prone buildings and other infrastructure. Geographical Information Systems (GIS) should be built to facilitate the quantification of near-term primary impacts as a first approximation of possible of future impacts.

Because sea level rise will be a global phenomenon, the geographical scale for identification and quantification of impacts should ideally be global. However, as previously discussed, the geographical scale related to policy-making will most often be the national scale (or lower). In effect, to determine the need for adaptive policy measures, assessment at a national (or even smaller) scale will do. But to determine the need for prevention in the first place, a global assessment will be necessary. A very tentative broad-brush global inventory of high risk areas is made by Delft Hydraulics (1989).

Monetary/Non-monetary Impacts

Impacts, both stochastic and non-stochastic, can be split up into monetary and non-monetary components. Monetary impacts have money as their normal "dimension of expression"; while non-monetary impacts are expressed in some other terms. Monetary impacts have prices associated with them, and are therefore approximated by the loss of goods and amenities that can be bought in the market-place. Obviously, non-monetary impacts cannot be valued in this way. Examples of non-monetary impacts would include: loss of human life; emotional stress due to a more dangerous situation; or the loss of a unique ecosystem (like the Waddensea in the Netherlands and the FRG).

Physical Norms, Risk Limits

Physical norms and risk limits are sometimes imposed, generally by exogenous forces. For instance, in the Netherlands a legal limit is set on the risk of flooding. In the Dutch case, the probability of flooding is decreed by law not to exceed one per cent per century. This particular risk limit was accepted by the Dutch Parliament after the severe flooding disaster which occurred in the Netherlands in 1953.

Where physical norms and standards do apply, further economic assessment may not be necessary if the projected sea level rise would lead to the decreed risk limit being exceeded. Policy measures would simply have to be taken to meet the limit. However, in most countries and for most types of impacts, no such limits have yet been formulated, so an economic assessment will normally be necessary.

Valuation

In the preceding sections, a distinction was made between monetary and non-monetary impacts. Monetary impacts relate to goods with a market price, and can therefore be valued relatively easily. Environmental impacts generally do not have a market price, and are therefore non-monetary. Not even all economic impacts can be expressed in monetary terms (e.g. employment). For decision- making purposes, it is also helpful to value non-monetary impacts, preferably in monetary terms. If a readily available price is missing, other valuing methods have to be used. Many techniques have been developed (and more are still being developed) for the valuation of environmental impacts.

Economic Assessment

As explained earlier, the model should first be run under the assumption of the "do nothing" policy. Using this assumption, damages due to potential SLR may be so high that some form of policy reaction will be required. In second and subsequent runs of the model, impacts will include the costs of these policy reactions. Conceptually, the only available economic method for comparing such policy alternatives is Cost Benefit Analysis (CBA). In CBA, all impacts are ideally expressed in monetary terms. If this requirement is not sufficiently met, a modified CBA-method can be applied, i.e. Multi-criteria Analysis (MCA). In MCA, impacts can be expressed in their own physical terms. It should, however, be noted that, either implicitly or explicitly, a subjective value judgement must also be made in MCA.

Some specific problems for the economic assessment phase of the work are discussed below.

Policy Measures

In Figure 3, a distinction is made between adaptive and preventive policy measures. Preventive measures will lead to a reduction of emission of greenhouse gases; these policy measures are outside the scope of this paper.

As noted earlier, adaptive responses can occur as a result of either private decisions or because of explicit public sector policies. Public sector adaptation may include such policies as construction of dikes and levees; disincentives for new investments in threatened areas; changes in the development zoning plans for threatened areas; or provision of additional infrastructure in areas which are less at risk from SLR.

Feedback loops connect public sector adaptive policies to the next round of identification of primary and secondary impacts. Obviously, one primary impact of a public policy will be the cost of that policy. Adaptive policy measures may also influence private adaptive behaviour, and therefore have effects on the level of secondary impacts.

COMPARISON OF POLICY ALTERNATIVES

When the framework described above is reiterated several times, a number of policy options will emerge and will have to be compared. The usual method for comparing these policy options is CBA or its modification, MCA.

The CBA model is most appropriate when it is marginal changes in economic activity that are being analysed. Over the long period of time between the beginning of the SLR problem and when its impacts are fully manifested, it is likely that changes (both physical and financial) will *not* be marginal, thereby calling into question the whole utility of the CBA model. However, the CBA approach is advocated here because: *1)* it is most readily understood by policy-makers; *2)* it is the best model available; and *3)* no reliable method of assessing relative price changes over a long period of time yet exists in any event. In addition, the price level change problem is likely to be small in practice, compared to the other uncertainties likely to be encountered in the assessment.

Another potential problem in assessing SLR policies is that links will exist between various policy areas. In other words, the impacts of SLR policy on other policy areas should also be taken into account in the assessment. This dynamic interaction between policy areas can be important. If, for instance, one policy option is to reduce CO_2 emissions, we might also expect benefits in terms of reduced acidification. These related impacts should not be overlooked. In the Netherlands, for example, dikes will have to be raised anyway, because the country is shifting slowly into the sea. Therefore, the cost of dike construction is not totally due to sea level rise policy, and the cost to be attributed to sea level rise policy is only the difference between construction now earlier and construction later. These links among policy areas obviously complicate the assessment of sea level rise policies.

In the remainder of this section, four other specific topics which complicate the assessment of SLR policies are discussed.

Uncertainty

The assessment of SLR policies depends on several assumptions, all of which are subject to uncertainty. Therefore, it should always be investigated whether or not the results of the assessment are robust with respect to these uncertainties. Uncertainties are introduced at four basic levels in the model: at the stage of the sea level rise scenario; at the stage of quantification of impacts; at the valuation stage; and at the implementation/effectiveness stage. These uncertainties may be large, usually due to the long term nature of the SLR problem. If the assessment is computerised, a Monte Carlo simulation could be used to investigate the sensitivity of the assessment with respect to the assumptions made (for treatment of Monte Carlo techniques, see e.g. Gardner *et al.*, 1983). An alternative method of sensitivity analysis is the calculation of turning points (thresholds), indicating where changes in the value of a particular variable cause the results of the assessment to change.

Sensitivity analysis is the only practical method available to investigate the influence of uncertainty on the result of an assessment. Through sensitivity analysis, it is also possible to determine key variables which are most relevant for the assessment. If one sees the key variables as the vectors determining the space of the assessment area, it would, in principle, be possible to divide this space into sub-areas, where certain policy alternatives are better than others. For example, let the policy alternatives be A1, A2 and A3, and let V1 and V2 be the (most) relevant variables subject to uncertainty, then it could be investigated where the alternatives are dominating the other alternatives, as depicted in Figure 7.

Figure 7. **DIVISION OF THE ASSESSMENT AREA ACCORDING TO PREFERRED POLICY ALTERNATIVES**

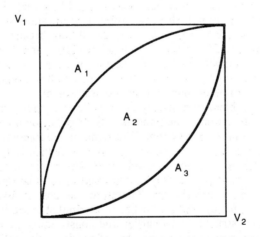

It should, however, be kept in mind that Figure 7 (like any other model) is a simplification. In reality, there will be more than two key variables subject to uncertainty, and there will usually be more than three policy options; the assessment area must therefore be multidimensional. It will remain difficult to determine which values of the variables are most probable, and which policy options are best. It should be acknowledged at the outset that there are no analytical methods which can remove basic uncertainties. Decision-making will simply have to be carried out in the face of this uncertainty.

Flexibility of Policies

Largely due to uncertainty, flexibility is a desirable feature of any policy measure. If, under certain assumptions about SLR, a given policy measure is assessed as the best one, it should then be investigated what the additional costs would be if SLR turned out to be higher than assumed, so that other measures would have to be taken. An inflexible policy measure is one that allows no add-on extensions, so that the measure would have to be replaced completely, if SLR turned out to be higher than originally assumed. A more flexible policy may be more expensive under a specific assumption about the level of SLR, but much cheaper if SLR will be higher. It may be worthwhile to buy some "insurance" by choosing a more flexible policy. In the design of policy measures, the maximum of flexibility commensurate with the additional costs involved should be the objective.

Intertemporal Comparison

Typically, the costs of both public and private action are incurred before the benefits of that action are realised. This time difference makes it difficult to compare costs and benefits when evaluating policy options. The usual method of handling this problem is to use a discounting procedure.

It has been argued that discounting is wrong for long-term environmental decision-making because: i) it unduly increases current rates of resource exploitation by discounting future benefits in the original investment decision; and ii) it undervalues future environmental damages that will result from present-day investment decisions.

The concept of sustainable development as enumerated by the Brundtland Commission (WCED, 1989), is a useful starting point for addressing this question. According to that body, "sustainable development is development that meets the needs of the present without compromising the ability of future generations to meet their needs". One way of achieving this objective might be to not discount at all in the case of irreversible environmental damage. But this would be the same as discounting at a rate of zero percent. Clearly, it would be better to recognise that a positive discount rate is necessary, and then to value future benefits and costs as realistically as possible. This would mean explicitly allowing future benefits and costs to incorporate all types of value. Specifically, it would mean that "existence", "bequest", and "option" values would be included as well as the more traditional "use" values.

It would also mean that future environmental damages likely to result from present decisions should be explicitly factored into the analysis.

Another key question involved in discounting concerns the specific rate(s) that should be used. In theory, the appropriate discount rate is the one where the social rate of time preference, (a "bribe" to entice consumers to delay present consumption), and the marginal productivity of capital, (a "bribe" to entice producers to invest), are in long-run equilibrium. But several things can cause these variables to be out of equilibrium. For example, the level of risk will vary from project to project, making different "bribes" necessary for some investments than for others. Also, macroeconomic policy (both monetary and fiscal) does not fall neutrally on all sectors, resulting in some being more profitable than others. Both of these factors mean that a long-run equilibrium discount rate will never be reached.

That being the case, what rate should be used? Without going into all the details here, the simple answer is that it depends on the source of the funds being used. If the source is "present consumption", then the appropriate rate is the social time preference rate. If the source of the funds is savings, then the appropriate rate to use is the marginal productivity of capital. Normally, we would expect the latter to be greater than the former. This is because of the existence of special taxes on capital, and because of the fact that higher risks are typically assumed by investors than by savers.

And finally, it should be recognised that "the" rate of social time preference is really an aggregation of individual consumers rates of time preference. There is no a priori reason why individual consumers should have the same rates of time preference for all resources.

All of the above suggest that it is probably appropriate to permit the use of different discount rates for different types of costs and benefits. A more detailed treatment of this question is provided in Pearce and Markyanda (1989).

Risk

Although risk and uncertainty are often discussed in the same breath, there is a clear distinction between the two. Risk involves probability, and uncertainty is just not-knowing. A risk can be well known in terms of probabilities and effects. Of course, risk and uncertainty may go together, when probabilities exist, but are not known.

Risk poses special problems in the economic assessment, especially in the case of risks associated with low probability - high consequences (e.g. flooding disasters). Evaluation of these risks through an 'expected value' approach (EV = probability * effect) will often not suffice. For monetary impacts, it can be argued that a hypothetical insurance premium is an acceptable valuation of risk. The insurance premium is hypothetical, because a State may act as its own insurance company. For events which occur relatively frequently, expected value is a guiding principle for insurance companies to determine the insurance premium. But for very low probabilities with very large effects, expected value will not be enough, and premiums will have to be much higher. Insurance companies usually try to spread risks using re-insurance schemes with other companies; and a consideration in the determination of the premium is that the insurance company will not go bankrupt in the case of a claim (Jansen, 1988). It is surprising that States, acting as their own insurance company, do not apply this practice of spreading risk with other States. Bankruptcy is not possible for States. To avoid disasters with large financial impacts, a State could also neutralise many of these impacts through an international loan. The interest on the loan would then be an upper-bound valuation of the impact; and the expected value would become a lower-bound valuation.

This logic does not apply to non-monetary impacts, since these cannot be neutralised through purchases on the open market. Some methods have been developed to monetarily value the risk to human life. For example, the U.S. Environmental Protection Agency (EPA) uses such monetary estimates in Regulatory Impact Assessments (RIAs). On the basis of wage differences in jobs with varying degrees of risk, a so-called statistical life is valued at $ 1-6 million. Obviously, there may be moral, ethical or philosophical objections to such valuation of human life. On the other hand, such valuation could lead to more consistency between different policy areas concerned with risks to human life. However, even if it is ultimately valued, damage to human life cannot be neutralised through purchases in the (international) markets. Therefore, risks with respect to non-monetary damages, whether or not monetarily valued, should always be described in physical terms too, so as to allow a comparison with a limit to risk (whether or not explicitly formulated).

VALUING IMPACTS

Damage due to sea level rise can be seen as a special case of damage due to environmental change in general. The special features of sea level rise, as compared to other types of environmental change, lie in the long-term aspects, intertemporal tradeoffs, and uncertainty and risk, rather than in the valuing of impacts *per se*. There is a fairly large body of literature on valuing environmental change, (see, for example, Freeman (1979), Pearce and Markandya (1989), Kuik *et al.*, (1989)). In this section, a short description of the general methodologies for valuing the impacts of environmental change is provided.

Damages due to environmental change can be assessed in both qualitative and quantitative ways. In a qualitative assessment, impacts that are likely to occur are identified and described, but are not quantified. This identification of impacts is a necessary first step in any assessment and can be very useful in a number of ways, e.g. to create public awareness that damage is likely to occur. For some environmental impacts of sea level rise, qualitative assessment is the best that can be expected at this moment, given our limited knowledge of complicated long term ecological processes.

If quantitative assessments are possible, they often give more useful information. Quantitative assessments can be subdivided into assessments in physical units (non-monetary) and in monetary units. Money is a convenient measuring rod for policy makers, but it is often not possible to place a meaningful and reliable monetary value on all impacts of environmental change. The wish to express all impacts in monetary terms rests partly on the presumption that politicians and government officials react most quickly to monetary data. This is questionable. For example, two widely accepted goals for macro-economic policy are full employment and a just distribution of income. Both goals are monitored in non-monetary terms, either in absolute numbers, poverty levels, percentage distribution, indices or coefficients. Likewise, if environmental quality is accepted as an appropriate policy goal, monetary measurement is not a necessary requirement.

However, if meaningful and reliable money values of damages can be calculated, decision-makers are provided with information that can, in a cost-benefit framework, be used to assess the merits of a particular policy. Table 5 provides a categorisation of available assessment methods. It distinguishes qualitative, quantitative (physical) and monetary assessment methods).

Table 5. **Assessment Methods**

---

1. Qualitative
2. Quantitative (physical)
3. Monetary
   3.1. Increased costs, increased outlays and productivity losses, measures in actual money transactions.
   3.2. Willingness to pay (including consumers' surpluses)
       3.2.1. based on market data
       3.2.2. based on derived market data (Travel Cost Method, Hedonic Approach)
       3.2.3. based on stated willingness to pay (Contingent Valuation Method)

In reviewing the state of the art in the Netherlands on the monetary valuation of environmental damage/benefits, Kuik *et al.*, (1989) concluded that available estimates lack comprehensiveness (i.e. value components like consumers' surplus, non-user values etc., are often not included) and completeness (i.e. not all impacts are included). Consequently, monetary estimates of environmental damages are generally downwards biased.

Non-monetary Quantitative Valuation

If no reliable monetary values can be derived for the impacts of environmental change, policy-makers will have to base their decisions on (preferably quantitative) information expressed in physical terms. In this case, the decision will usually not be based on a rigid CBA assessment.

In this case, Multi Criteria Analysis provides a number of techniques which *do* allow a systematic assessment, even if not all impacts are expressed in monetary terms. In MCA, statistical weighting techniques are used to rank policy alternatives, with impacts measured in their own dimensions (e.g. safety from flooding expressed in terms of probability and number of people; expected loss of wetlands in terms of hectares; cost of coastal defence measures in monetary terms). Admittedly, some value judgements are still required in MCA, be it implicitly or explicitly.

To compensate for these bases, emphasis should be placed on sensitivity analysis, in order to examine the effects of uncertainties and different weighting schemes on the ranking of the policy alternatives. As a rule, MCA does not provide the decision-maker with a unique solution to his decision problem, but it can give some guidance in difficult multidimensional tradeoffs. Several examples of the theory and application of MCA can be found in Keeney and Raiffa (1976), Zeleny (1982), Voogd (1983), Steuer (1986), and Janssen (1989).

Monetary Valuation

Direct Valuation

Direct valuation is based on market prices and actual monetary transactions. Direct valuation can be used to value the costs of coastal defence systems; costs of abatement of beach erosion; increased outlays to maintain or improve the drinking water supplies; loss of buildings and other infrastructure; decreases in agricultural crops due to salt intrusion; etc. If a market is not functioning in such a way that it sufficiently or accurately reflects actual scarcities, shadow pricing may be needed. For instance, in a situation of large unemployment, labour costs may be valued at zero.

Willingness to Pay

Methods based on willingness to pay (WTP) are based on individuals' preferences. For example, the market price of a particular house is determined by the forces of demand and supply. The utility (or welfare) in money terms, an owner derives from this house can be larger than the market price. He or she was perhaps willing to pay more for the house than the going market price (not less, because then he or she would not have bought the house). The actual loss of welfare in case of loss of the house is then larger than the market price. The difference between the market price and the willingness to pay is known as the consumer's surplus.

For goods and services that are bought and sold on markets (like houses), WTP estimates can be made with the help of demand curves that are based on market transaction data. For goods and services that are not traded in markets (like valuable wetlands, recreational beaches, coastal defence) no direct market data are available to estimate WTP. To value these goods and services, several alternative methods have been developed.

The *Travel Cost Method* (TCM) was developed to estimate the value of free recreational amenities (like beaches). The idea behind this method is to use information on money and time that individuals spend in getting to a particular site to estimate a hypothetical demand curve for that site. The WTP for the facilities at that site is equal to the area under the demand curve.

The *Hedonic Approach* is based on the assumption that the attractiveness of an asset is determined by a particular set of attributes. By using statistical techniques, the implied values of these attributes can be assessed. For example, the attractiveness of a house is influenced by the environmental quality of its location. The price difference between houses that differ only in environmental quality, yields an implied value of that environmental quality. The wage difference between jobs with different risks attached to them, but are otherwise equal, can be seen as an implicit value of that risk. The wage differential method has sometimes been applied to estimate the value of policy measures that reduce environmental risks to human health.

The *Contingent Valuation Method* (CVM) is based on a hypothetical market. The method employs survey techniques to infer individuals' willingness to pay for a well-defined environmental improvement so as to estimate the shape of a hypothetical demand curve. In

Table 6. **Monetary Valuation Methods, Applicable to Impacts**

impact category	receptor/effect	linkage to welfare	valuation method
Reproduceable stocks	building	maintenance + repair	increased outlays
	infrastructure	maintenance + repair	increased outlays
	materials	maintenance + repair	increased outlays
	coastal defence	maintenance + repair	increased outlays
	beaches	maintenance + repair	increased outlays
		recreation	TCM, CVM, hedonic approach
Reproduceable flows	economic sectors	loss of crops, fisheries, economic activity	decreased productivity
	drinking water	buffering, purification	increased outlays
Non reproduceable stocks	historic monuments	restauration	increased outlays
	ecosystems	recreation	CVM, TCM, hedonic approach
		non-user values	CVM
Human healts, wellbeing	illness	work days lost	decreased productivity
		pain + suffering	CVM, hedinic wage
		medical care	increased outlays
	risk of flooding	house prices	hedonic approach
	mortality	work days lost	decrease productivity
		risk of death	hedonic wage
		medical care	increased outlays

103

the United Kingdom, a CVM approach has been used to estimate the value of a recreational beach on the south coast (Hastings) threatened by coastal erosion (see: Coker et al., 1989).

CVM is the only method which also attempts to value non-user values. Non-user value is the value people attach to goods and amenities even if they may never make use of them. Three types are distinguished. "Option value" is the value people attach to a good or amenity in order to keep the option open to use them in the future. "Existence" value is the value people attach to amenities for its intrinsic value, e.g. a piece of nature that has no economic value, not even for recreational purposes. "Bequest value" expresses the wish to conserve goods and amenities for future generations. Non-user values are believed to be especially important for managing natural resources, because of the typically long term nature of decisions affecting these resources.

In Table 6, impacts are listed with applicable valuation methods. For a more thorough description and evaluation of the various valuation methods, see Pearce and Markandya (1989).

CONCLUSIONS AND RECOMMENDATIONS

Conclusions

Several conclusions about assessing the SLR impacts of climate change seem plausible, based on this study:

- Preventive policy measures should be implemented at a global scale and will be effective only in the very long run. Adaptive policy measures can more easily be implemented at a national or local scale. In most cases, policy-makers will not have the luxury of waiting until preventive measures can become effective. Therefore, there will most often not be a pure trade-off between preventive and adaptive policy measures;
- It is not entirely possible to isolate the impacts of sea level rise from the other consequences of climatic change, due to dynamic interactions among variables. However, it is possible to focus on sea level rise as a separate policy problem. When assessing policy measures to offset sea level rise problems, it is important to remember that other policy areas may also be affected. The impacts of SLR response policy measures on other policy areas should not be overlooked;
- To date, not many studies have been carried out with respect to the economic assessment of sea level rise, and those which have been done have taken an "engineering" approach, (merely estimating the costs of engineering defence measures). Much less attention has been given to behavioural adaptations and to non-financial damages (e.g. ecosystems);
- The availability of data with respect to altitudes of vulnerable areas and to the presently existing buildings and infrastructure differs widely among countries;
- Any assessment of sea level rise impacts is subject to large uncertainties. For example, no consensus yet exists on either the extent or the rate of sea level rise. Uncertainties also arise when impacts are quantified or modelled. Finally, uncertainties exist with respect to behavioural adaptations. These uncertainties are exacerbated by the long term nature of the sea level rise problem;
- Intertemporal and intergenerational trade-offs are always a problem when assessing long term phenomena. So far, the only practical way to make this trade-off is to

use a discount rate. Because several factors play a role in establishing an appropriate discount rate, there is no necessity to use the same rate to discount all impacts;
- Valuing the risk of non-monetary damages is another problem. Differences between perceived risk and statistical risk play a role. A possible solution might be a contingent valuation approach. Formulated risk limits can help in assessing risks, but it should be recalled that the assessment of a risk limit itself runs again into the valuation problem;
- The monetary valuation of non-monetary impacts (such as environmental impacts) is very difficult. Moreover, this type of monetary estimate has a structural tendency to a downward bias. Where monetary valuation problems impede a strict Cost Benefit Analysis, Multi Criteria Analysis may provide an alternative;
- Non-user values (option value, bequest value, existence value) are probably a substantial component of the value of assets which will be affected by sea level rise. The Contingency Valuation Method (CVM) is the only valuation method which comprises non-user values, and it seems to offer some promise for expanded use in this type of environmental analysis for the future.

Recommendations

- Future case studies on the impacts of sea level rise should combine the engineering approach with an approach which takes private adaptative behaviour into consideration;
- Geographic Information Systems should be set up and expanded, to help fill part of the information gap which presently exists in the SLR impact assessment field;
- Monetary valuation will, in many cases, be rather unreliable. It is therefore recommended that impacts of sea level rise be stated in their own dimension, even when a monetary value is also estimated;
- In view of the large uncertainties involved in assessing impacts, sensitivity analysis should always be undertaken. Sensitivity analysis is also feasible when using the MCA approach. A case study should be undertaken (using MCA) to investigate which policy alternatives are preferable at different values of key (uncertain) variables;
- SLR Policy analysis should investigate at least a "low" scenario of SLR, so as to identify the minimal policy measures required. A "high" scenario should also be included, so as to assess whether it is feasible to delay implementing policy measures until more certainty exists about the SLR problem and potential solutions;
- The political acceptability of CVM is still rather low, due to its supposed unreliability. Because CVM does not contain the downward bias of other valuation methods, ways should be sought to stimulate its political acceptability;
- Flexibility of policy measures should be aimed for in the policy design stage. Flexibility should also be taken into account when assessing policy options;
- In developed countries, impacts on tourism might be among the most important impacts of sea level rise. Because this type of impact has been virtually ignored in existing case studies, future case studies in this subject area should be undertaken;
- Using a "broad-brush" approach, countries should inventory which areas are most vulnerable with respect to SLR. Guided by the results of this inventory, more detailed case studies for assessment of impacts and of policy measures should then be carried out.

REFERENCES

ATMOSPHERIC ENVIRONMENT SERVICE, ATLANTIC REGION, ENVIRONMENT CANADA (1986). *Preliminary Study of the Possible Impacts of a One-metre Rise In Sea Level at Charlottetown, Prince Edward Island.* Report prepared by P. Lane and Associates Limited, Halifax, Nova Scotia.

ATMOSPHERIC ENVIRONMENT SERVICE - ONTARIO REGION, ENVIRONMENT CANADA (1986). *CO2-Induced Climate Change in Ontario-Interdependencies and Potential Resource and Socio-Economic Strategies.*

ATMOSPHERIC ENVIRONMENT SERVICE, ATLANTIC REGION, ENVIRONMENT CANADA (1987). *Effects of a One-metre Sea-level Rise at Saint John, New Brunswick and the Lower Reaches of the Saint John River.* Report prepared by Martec Limited, Halifax, Nova Scotia.

BEE, C., FURLER, W. QUINN, N. *Greenhouse: International and National Policy Approaches.*

BERZ, G. *Climatic Change: Impact On International Reinsurance.*

BLOK, K., HENDRIKS, C., TURKENBURG, W. *The Role of Carbon Dioxide Removal in the Reduction of the Greenhouse Effect.* Dept. of Science, Technology and Society, University of Utrecht (ed).

BODELL, R., GRIMA, A.P., TIMMERMAN, P. (1987). *Economic Perspectives on the Impact of Climate Variability and Change.* The Inter-university Working Group on Economics and Climate Change (ed.).

BROADUS, J.M., SOLOW, A.R. (1988). "Towards a Policy for Global Climate Change". In: *AERE Newsletter.*

BROWN, L.R., *et al.* (1988). *State of the World,* W.W. Norton Company, New York, London.

BROWN, L.R., *et al.* (1989). *State of the World,* W.W. Norton Company, New York, London.

BRYANT, E. *Sea-level Variability and its Impact Within the Greenhouse Scenario.*

COMMISSION OF THE EUROPEAN COMMUNITIES (1988). *Communication to the Council: The Greenhouse Effect and the Community.* Commission work programme concerning the evaluation of policy options to deal with the "greenhouse effect" and Draft Council Resolution, Brussels.

COKER, A.M., THOMPSON, P.M., SMITH, D.I., PENNING-ROWSELL. E.C. (1989). *The Impact of Climate Change on Coastal Zone Management in Britain: a Preliminary Analysis.*

DELFT HYDRAULICS (ed.) (1989). *Criteria for Assessing Vulnerability to Sea-Level Rise: A Global Inventory for High Risk Areas.*

DELFT HYDRAULICS (ed.) (1988). *Impact of Sea Level Rise on Society. A Case Study for the Netherlands.*

DALTACOMMISSIE (1960). *Report of the Delta Commission.*

DE RONDE, J.G. (1987). *Impact of Sea-Level Rise on a Low-Lying Country Like the Netherlands.* Workshop Noordwijkerhout.

DIE ZEIT (1989). *Das Nebul se Treibhaus*, No. 39, 22 September 1989.

ELZEN, M.G.J. DEN, ROTMANS, J. (1988). *Simulatiemodel Voor Een Aantal Maatschappelijke Gevolgen Van Het Broeikaseffect Voor Nederland.* RIVM.

EMBER, L.R., LAYMAN, P.L., LEPKOWSKI, W., ZURER, P.S. (1986). "Tending the Global Commons". In: *Chemical and Engineering News,* Washington, pp. 14-48, Vol. 64.

ENVIRONMENTAL AGENCY, GOVERNMENT OF JAPAN (1988). *Policy Recommendations Concerning Climate Change.*

ETTINGER, J. VAN, JANSEN, T.H., JEPMA, C.J. (1989). *Climate, Environment and Development.* Paper for the Ministerial Conference on Atmospheric Pollution and Climate Change, Den Haag.

FOWLER, R.J., *Policy and Legal Implications of the Greenhouse-Effect.*

GARDNER, R., ROJDER, B., U. BERGSTROM (1983). *PRISM - A Systematic Method for Determining the Effect of Parameter Uncertainties on Model Predictions.* Studsvik Energiteknik A.B., Nykoping, Sweden.

GIBBS, M.J. (1984). "Economic Analysis of Sea Level Rise: Methods and Results". In: Barth, M.C., Titus, J.G. (eds.) (1984). *Greenhouse Effect and Sea Level Rise, A Challenge for this Generation,* Van Nostrand Reinhold, New York.

HEKSTRA, G. (1986). "Will Climate Change Flood the Netherlands? Effects on Agriculture, Land-Use and Well-Being". In: *Ambio,* Vol. 15, No. 6, pp. 316-326.

HEKSTRA, G.P., (1989). "Global Warming and Rising Sea Levels: The Policy Implications". *The Ecologist,* Vol. 19, No. 1, pp. 4-15.

HOFFMAN, J.S., KEYES, D., TITUS J.G., *Projecting Future Sea Level Rise - Methodology, Estimates to the Year 2100, and Research Needs.* United States Environmental Protection Agency (ed), 2nd Edition.

HOUGHTON, R.A., WOODWELL, G.M. (1989). "Global Climatic Change". In: *Scientific American,* Vol. 260, No. 4.

HOURCADE, J.C., MEGIE, G., THEYS, D. *Modifications Climatiques et Réorientation des Politiques Énergétiques: Comment Gérer L'incertitude?* 14e congrès de la conférence mondiale de l'énergie.

INTERNATIONAL CONFERENCE ON THE CHANGING ATMOSPHERE (1988). *The Changing Atmosphere: Implications for Global Security.* Conference statement, Toronto.

JANSEN, H.M.A. (1988). *Financieel-Economisch Risico Limiet.* Ministry of Public Housing, Physical Planning and Environmental Management.

JANSSEN, R. (1989, in press). "DEFINITE, A System to Support the Decision-Making Process". In: *Anon, Decision-Aiding Software and Decision Analysis*, Cambridge University Press, Cambridge.

JELGERSMA, S., TOOLEY, M.J., SHENNAN, I. (1987). *The Impacts of a Future Rise in Sea Level on the European Lowlands.* Paper for the European workshop on interrelated bioclimatic and land use chances. Noordwijkerhout, the Netherlands.

KEENEY, R.L., RAIFFA, H. (1976). *Decisions with Multiple Objectives; Preferences and Value Trade-offs.* Wiley, New York.

KLAASSEN, G., JANSEN, H.M.A. (1989). *Economic Principles for Reducing Sulphur Emissions in Europe.* UN-ECE (restricted).

KUIK, O.J., JANSEN, H.M.A., OPSCHOOR, J.B. (1989). *Environmental Benefit Estimates in Decision-Making in the Netherlands.* OECD, Paris.

LASHOF, D.A., TIRPAK, D.A. (1989). *Policy Options for Stabilising Global Climate.* Draft. US Environmental Protection Agency (ed.).

LIEHNE, P.F.S. *Climatic Influences on Mosquito-borne Diseases in Australia.*

LOVE, G. *Cyclone Storm Surges: Post Greenhouse.*

LOWE, I. *The Energy Policy Implications of Climate Change.*

MALDE, J. VAN (1987). *Relative Rise of Mean Sea Levels in the Netherlands in Recent Times.* Workshop Noordwijkerhout.

MANNE, A.S., RICHELS, R.J. (1989). *CO2 Emission Limits: An Economic Analysis for the USA.* Draft.

MARINO, M.G. (1987). *Carbon Dioxide Build-up: Impact on Western Mediterranean. The Ebro Delta Case.* Workshop Noordwijkerhout.

MARTA, T.J. (1988). *Social Implication of Climate Change: A Review of the Canadian Perspective.* Environment Canada, Inland Waters, Directorate Water Planning and Management Branch, Ottawa, Canada.

MERCER, D.C., PETERSON, J.A. *Australia and the Greenhouse Effect: The Science/Policy Debate.*

MINTZER, J. (1989). "Cooling Down a Warming World - Chlorofluorocarbons, the Greenhouse Effect, and the Montreal Protocol". In: *International Environmental Affairs: A Journal for Research and Policy*, Vol. 1, No. 1.

NORDHAUS, W.D. (1989). *The Economics of the Greenhouse Effect.*

PEARCE, D., MARKANDYA, A. (1989). *Environmental Policy Benefits. Monetary Valuation.* OECD, Paris.

ROTMANS, J., DE BOOIS, H., SWART, R.J., *An Integrated Model for the Assessment of the Greenhouse Effect: The Dutch approach.*

RIND, D. (1989). "A Character Sketch of Greenhouse". In: *EPA Journal*, Vol. 15, No. 1.

SASSIN, W. (1989). *Decision Under Uncertainty, A Frame for Evaluating Various Contributions to Climatic Change and Related Response Strategies*, Paris.

SESTINI, G. (1987). *The Impact of Sea-Level and Temperature Increases on the Deltaic Lowlands of the Eastern Mediterranean.* Workshop Noordwijkerhout.

SHENNAN, J., TOOLEY, M.J. *Conspectus of Fundamental and Strategic Research on Sea-Level Changes.*

SIGBJARNARSON, G. (ed.) (1985). *Future Global Warming and Sea Level Rise.* By: J.S. Hoffman, J.B. Wells, J.G. Titus; papers presented at Symposium on Coastal Geomorphology Sedimentary Budgets Coastal and River Hydraulics, Reykjavik, Iceland.

SMITH, J.B., TIRPAK, D.A. (1988). *The Potential Effect of Global Climate Change on the United States.* United States Environmental Protection Agency (ed). Draft Report to the Congress.

STEUER, R.E. (1986). *Multiple Criteria Optimisation: Theory, Computation and Application.* Wiley, New York.

STOKOE, P.K., LEBLANC, M. (1987). *Socio-Economic Assessment of the Physical and Ecological Impacts of Climate Change on the Marine Environment of the Atlantic Region of Canada.* School for Resource and Environmental Studies, Dalhousie University, Nova Scotia, Canada.

SWART, R., ROMANS, J. (1989). *Climate Change or Climate Chance?* RIVM (ed.). Paper presented at the International Energy Workshop, Laxenburg, Austria.

TATA ENERGY RESEARCH INSTITUTE (1986). *Conference Statement: International Conference on Global Warming and Climate Change: Perspectives from Developing Countries.* Organised in association with The Woods Hole Research Centre, Woods Hole, Massachusetts, USA and New Delhi, India.

TIRPAK, D.A. (1986). "Potential Effects of Future Climate Changes on Forest and Vegetation, Agriculture, Water Resources, and Human Health". In: EPA (1987) *Assessing the Risks of Trace Gases that can Modify the Stratosphere*, Vol. V, Appendix B.

TITUS, J.G. (1986). "Greenhouse Effect, Sea Level Rise and Coastal Zone Management". In: *Coastal Zone Management Journal*, Vol. 14, No. 3.

TITUS, J.G. (1986). "Sea Level Rise, Draft". In *Effects of Changes in Stratospheric Ozone and Global Climate*, Vol. 4.

TITUS, J.G., BARTH, M.C. (1984). "An Overview of the Causes and Effects of Sea Level Rise". In: *Greenhouse Effect and Sea Level Rise, A Challenge for this Generation*, Van Nostrand Reinhold, New York.

TURNER, R.K., DENT, D., HEY, R.D., (1983). "Valuation of the Environmental Impact of Wetland Flood Protection and Drainage Schemes". In: *Environment and Planning*, Vol. 15, pp. 871-888.

UK DEPARTMENT OF ENVIRONMENT (1988). *Possible Impacts of Climate Change on the Natural Environment in the United Kingdom*, London.

VAN DE VEEN, H. (1989). "Het Verdronken land van 2050". Uit: *Onze Wereld*.

VELLINGA, P. (1987). "Sea Level Rise, Consequences and Policies". In: SCHRODER, P.C. (ed.), *Sea Level Rise, A Selective Retrospection*.

VOOGD, H. (1983). *Multicriteria Evaluation for Urban and Regional Planning*, Pion, London.

WEGGEL, J.R., ASCE, F. (1986). "Economics of Beach Nourishment Under Scenario of Rising Sea Level". In: *Journal of Waterway, Port, Coastal and Ocean Engineering*, Vol. 112, pp. 418-426, New York.

WILLEM, W.J. (September 1987). *The Environmental Protection Policy in the Netherlands Towards Agricultural Impacts on Soil and Groundwater;* European Conference: Impact of Agriculture on Water Resources.

WIND, H.G. (ed.) (1987). *Impact of Sea Level Rise on Society*. A.A. Balkema, Rotterdam.

WORLD COMMISSION OF ENVIRONMENT AND DEVELOPMENT (1987). *Our Common Future*. Oxford University Press.

WRIGHT, J. (1989). *Future Generations and the Environment*. Centre for Resource Management, New Zealand.

ZAZO, C., GOY, J.L., DABRIO, J.C. (1987). *Late Quaternary and Recent Evolution of Coastal Morphology of the Gulf of Cadiz (Huelva-Cadiz), South-western Spain*. Workshop Noordwijkerhout.

ZELENY, M. (1982). *Multiple Criteria Decision Making*. McGraw Hill, New York.

ZWERVER, S., R. SWART, A.P. VAN ULDEN (1989). *Een Paar Graden Meer? Achtergronden en Ontwikkelingen Van Het Broeikaseffect Door CO2*. RIVM/KNMI, Bilthoven, The Netherlands.

WHERE TO OBTAIN OECD PUBLICATIONS – OÙ OBTENIR LES PUBLICATIONS DE L'OCDE

Argentina – Argentine
Carlos Hirsch S.R.L.
Galería Güemes, Florida 165, 4° Piso
1333 Buenos Aires   Tel. 30.7122, 331.1787 y 331.2391
Telegram: Hirsch–Baires
Telex: 21112 UAPE–AR. Ref. s/2901
Telefax:(1)331–1787

Australia – Australie
D.A. Book (Aust.) Pty. Ltd.
648 Whitehorse Road, P.O.B 163
Mitcham, Victoria 3132   Tel. (03)873.4411
Telex: AA37911 DA BOOK
Telefax: (03)873.5679

Austria – Autriche
OECD Publications and Information Centre
Schedestrasse 7
5300 Bonn 1 (Germany)   Tel. (0228)21.60.45
Telefax: (0228)26.11.04

Gerold & Co.
Graben 31
Wien I   Tel. (0222)533.50.14

Belgium – Belgique
Jean De Lannoy
Avenue du Roi 202
B–1060 Bruxelles   Tel. (02)538.51.69/538.08.41
Telex: 63220   Telefax: (02) 538.08.41

Canada
Renouf Publishing Company Ltd.
1294 Algoma Road
Ottawa, ON K1B 3W8   Tel. (613)741.4333
Telex: 053–4783   Telefax: (613)741.5439
Stores:
61 Sparks Street
Ottawa, ON K1P 5R1   Tel. (613)238.8985
211 Yonge Street
Toronto, ON M5B 1M4   Tel. (416)363.3171

Federal Publications
165 University Avenue
Toronto, ON M5H 3B8   Tel. (416)581.1552
Telefax: (416)581.1743

Les Publications Fédérales
1185 rue de l'Université
Montréal, PQ H3B 3A7   Tel.(514)954–1633

Les Éditions La Liberté Inc.
3020 Chemin Sainte–Foy
Sainte–Foy, PQ G1X 3V6   Tel. (418)658.3763
Telefax: (418)658.3763

Denmark – Danemark
Munksgaard Export and Subscription Service
35, Norre Sogade, P.O. Box 2148
DK–1016 København K   Tel. (45 33)12.85.70
Telex: 19431 MUNKS DK   Telefax: (45 33)12.93.87

Finland – Finlande
Akateeminen Kirjakauppa
Keskuskatu 1, P.O. Box 128
00100 Helsinki   Tel. (358 0)12141
Telex: 125080   Telefax: (358 0)121.4441

France
OECD/OCDE
Mail Orders/Commandes par correspondance:
2 rue André–Pascal
75775 Paris Cedex 16   Tel. (1)45.24.82.00
Bookshop/Librairie:
33, rue Octave–Feuillet
75016 Paris   Tel. (1)45.24.81.67
   (1)45.24.81.81
Telex: 620 160 OCDE
Telefax: (33–1)45.24.85.00

Librairie de l'Université
12a, rue Nazareth
13090 Aix–en–Provence   Tel. 42.26.18.08

Germany – Allemagne
OECD Publications and Information Centre
Schedestrasse 7
5300 Bonn 1   Tel. (0228)21.60.45
Telefax: (0228)26.11.04

Greece – Grèce
Librairie Kauffmann
28 rue du Stade
105 64 Athens   Tel. 322.21.60
Telex: 218187 LIKA Gr

Hong Kong
Swindon Book Co. Ltd.
13 – 15 Lock Road
Kowloon, Hongkong   Tel. 366 80 31
Telex: 50 441 SWIN HX
Telefax: 739 49 75

Iceland – Islande
Mál Mog Menning
Laugavegi 18, Pósthólf 392
121 Reykjavik   Tel. 15199/24240

India – Inde
Oxford Book and Stationery Co.
Scindia House
New Delhi 110001   Tel. 331.5896/5308
Telex: 31 61990 AM IN
Telefax: (11)332.5993
17 Park Street
Calcutta 700016   Tel. 240832

Indonesia – Indonésie
Pdii–Lipi
P.O. Box 269/JKSMG/88
Jakarta 12790   Tel. 583467
Telex: 62 875

Ireland – Irlande
TDC Publishers – Library Suppliers
12 North Frederick Street
Dublin 1   Tel. 744835/749677
Telex: 33530 TDCP El Telefax : 748416

Italy – Italie
Libreria Commissionaria Sansoni
Via Benedetto Fortini, 120/10
Casella Post. 552
50125 Firenze   Tel. (055)645415
Telex: 570466   Telefax: (39.55)641257
Via Bartolini 29
20155 Milano   Tel. 365083
La diffusione delle pubblicazioni OCSE viene assicurata dalle
principali librerie ed anche da:
Editrice e Libreria Herder
Piazza Montecitorio 120
00186 Roma   Tel. 679.4628
Telex: NATEL I 621427
Libreria Hoepli
Via Hoepli 5
20121 Milano   Tel. 865446
Telex: 31.33.95 Telefax: (39.2)805.2886
Libreria Scientifica
Dott. Lucio de Biasio "Aeiou"
Via Meravigli 16
20123 Milano   Tel. 807679
Telefax: 800175

Japan– Japon
OECD Publications and Information Centre
Landic Akasaka Building
2–3–4 Akasaka, Minato–ku
Tokyo 107   Tel. (81.3)3586.2016
Telefax: (81.3)3584.7929

Korea – Corée
Kyobo Book Centre Co. Ltd.
P.O. Box 1658, Kwang Hwa Moon
Seoul   Tel. (REP)730.78.91
Telefax: 735.0030

Malaysia/Singapore – Malaisie/Singapour
Co–operative Bookshop Ltd.
University of Malaya
P.O. Box 1127, Jalan Pantai Baru
59700 Kuala Lumpur
Malaysia   Tel. 756.5000/756.5425
Telefax: 757.3661

Information Publications Pte. Ltd.
Pei–Fu Industrial Building
24 New Industrial Road No. 02–06
Singapore 1953   Tel. 283.1786/283.1798
Telefax: 284.8875

Netherlands – Pays–Bas
SDU Uitgeverij
Christoffel Plantijnstraat 2
Postbus 20014
2500 EA's–Gravenhage   Tel. (070)78.99.11
Voor bestellingen: Tel. (070 3)78.98.80
Telex: 32486 stdru   Telefax: (070 3)47.63.51

New Zealand – Nouvelle–Zélande
Government Printing Office
Customer Services
33 The Esplanade – P.O. Box 38–900
Petone, Wellington
Tel. (04) 685–555   Telefax: (04)685–333

Norway – Norvège
Narvesen Info Center – NIC
Bertrand Narvesens vei 2
P.O. Box 6125 Etterstad
0602 Oslo 6   Tel. (02)57.33.00
Telex: 79668 NIC N   Telefax: (02)68.19.01

Pakistan
Mirza Book Agency
65 Shahrah Quaid–E–Azam
Lahore 3   Tel. 66839
Telex: 44886 UBL PK. Attn: MIRZA BK

Portugal
Livraria Portugal
Rua do Carmo 70–74
Apart. 2681
1117 Lisboa Codex   Tel. 347.49.82/3/4/5
Telefax: 37 02 64

Singapore/Malaysia – Singapour/Malaisie
See "Malaysia/Singapore – "Voir "Malaisie/Singapour"

Spain – Espagne
Mundi–Prensa Libros S.A.
Castelló 37, Apartado 1223
Madrid 28001   Tel. (91) 431.33.99
Telex: 49370 MPLI   Telefax: 575 39 98
Libreria Internacional AEDOS
Consejo de Ciento 391
08009 –Barcelona   Tel. (93) 301–86–15
Telefax: (93) 317–01–41

Sweden – Suède
Fritzes Fackboksföretaget
Box 16356, S 103 27 STH
Regeringsgatan 12
DS Stockholm   Tel. (08)23.89.00
Telex: 12387 Telefax: (08)20.50.21

Subscription Agency/Abonnements:
Wennergren–Williams AB
Nordenflychtsvagen 74
Box 30004
104 25 Stockholm   Tel. (08)13.67.00
Telex: 19937 Telefax: (08)618.62.36

Switzerland – Suisse
OECD Publications and Information Centre
Schedestrasse 7
5300 Bonn 1 (Germany)   Tel. (0228)21.60.45
Telefax: (0228)26.11.04

Librairie Payot
6 rue Grenus
1211 Genève 11   Tel. (022)731.89.50
Telex: 28356
Subscription Agency – Service des Abonnements
4 place Pépinet – BP 3312
1002 Lausanne   Tel. (021)341.33.31
Telefax: (021)341.33.45
Maditec S.A.
Ch. des Palettes 4
1020 Renens/Lausanne   Tel. (021)635.08.65
Telefax: (021)635.07.80
United Nations Bookshop/Librairie des Nations–Unies
Palais des Nations
1211 Genève 10   Tel. (022)734.60.11 (ext. 48.72)
Telex: 289696 (Attn: Sales)
Telefax: (022)733.98.79

Taiwan – Formose
Good Faith Worldwide Int'l. Co. Ltd.
9th Floor, No. 118, Sec. 2
Chung Hsiao E. Road
Taipei   Tel. 391.7396/391.7397
Telefax: (02) 394.9176

Thailand – Thaïlande
Suksit Siam Co. Ltd.
1715 Rama IV Road, Samyan
Bangkok 5   Tel. 251.1630

Turkey – Turquie
Kültur Yayinlari Is–Türk Ltd. Sti.
Atatürk Bulvari No. 191/Kat. 21
Kavaklidere/Ankara   Tel. 25.07.60
Dolmabahce Cad. No. 29
Besiktas/Istanbul   Tel. 160.71.88
Telex: 43482B

United Kingdom – Royaume–Uni
HMSO
Gen. enquiries   Tel. (071) 873 0011
Postal orders only:
P.O. Box 276, London SW8 5DT
Personal Callers HMSO Bookshop
49 High Holborn, London WC1V 6HB
Telex: 297138 Telefax: 071 873 8463
Branches at: Belfast, Birmingham, Bristol, Edinburgh,
Manchester

United States – États–Unis
OECD Publications and Information Centre
2001 L Street N.W., Suite 700
Washington, D.C. 20036–4095   Tel. (202)785.6323
Telefax: (202)785.0350

Venezuela
Libreria del Este
Avda F. Miranda 52, Aptdo. 60337
Edificio Galipán
Caracas 106   Tel. 951.1705/951.2307/951.1297
Telegram: Libreste Caracas

Yugoslavia – Yougoslavie
Jugoslovenska Knjiga
Knez Mihajlova 2, P.O. Box 36
Beograd   Tel. (011)621.992
Telex: 12466 jk bgd   Telefax: (011)625.970

Orders and inquiries from countries where Distributors have
not yet been appointed should be sent to: OECD Publications
Service, 2 rue André–Pascal, 75775 Paris Cedex 16, France.
Les commandes provenant de pays où l'OCDE n'a pas encore
désigné de distributeur devraient être adressées à : OCDE,
Service des Publications, 2, rue André–Pascal, 75775 Paris
Cedex 16, France.

LES ÉDITIONS DE L'OCDE, 2, rue André-Pascal, 75775 PARIS CEDEX 16
IMPRIMÉ EN FRANCE
(97 90 02 2) ISBN 92-64-23462-4 - N° 45416 1991